Penguin Education
Penguin English Project Stage

I Took my Mind a Walk
Edited by George Sanders

Chairman: Patrick Radley

Other Worlds
Edited by Donald Ball

Things Working
Edited by Penny Blackie

Family and School
Edited by David Jackson

Ventures
Edited by Elwyn Rowlands

I Took my Mind a Walk
Edited by George Sanders

Creatures Moving
Edited by Geoffrey Summerfield

Penguin English Projec

Edited by George Sanders

Stage One **I Took my Mind a Walk**

Penguin Books

Penguin Books Ltd, Harmondsworth,
Middlesex, England
Penguin Books Australia Ltd,
Ringwood, Victoria, Australia

First published 1971
This selection copyright © George Sanders, 1971

Set in Monophoto Ehrhardt by
Oliver Burridge Filmsetting Ltd, Crawley, England
Printed in Great Britain by
George Pulman and Sons Ltd,
Watling Street, Bletchley, Bucks

Contents

An Ordinary Day

I took my mind a walk
Or my mind took me a walk –
Whichever was the truth of it.

The light glittered on the water
Or the water glittered in the light.
Cormorants stood on a tidal rock

With their wings spread out,
Stopping no traffic. Various ducks
Shilly-shallied here and there

On the shilly-shallying water.
An occasional gull yelped. Small flowers
Were doing their level best

To bring to their kerb bees like
Aerial charabancs. Long weeds in the clear
Water did Eastern dances, unregarded

By shoals of darning needles. A cow
Started a moo but thought
Better of it. . . . And my feet took me home

And my mind observed to me,
Or I to it, how ordinary
Extraordinary things are or

How extraordinary ordinary
Things are, like the nature of the mind
And the process of observing.

Norman MacCaig

Artist's Notebook

If you throw a stone into a pond with differently shaped shores all the waves which strike against these shores are thrown back towards the spot where the stone struck; and on meeting other waves they never intercept each other's course . . . a wave produced in a small pond will go and return many times to the spot where it originated. . . . Only in high seas do waves advance without recoil. In small ponds one and the same stroke gives birth to many motions of advance and recoil. The greater wave is covered with innumerable other waves which move in different directions; and these are deep or shallow according to the power that generated them. . . . Many waves turned in different directions can be created between the surface and the bottom of the same body of water at the same time . . . all the impressions caused by things striking upon the water can penetrate one another without being destroyed. One wave never penetrates another; but they only recoil from the spot where they strike.

The spiral or rotary movement of every liquid is swifter in proportion as it is nearer to the centre of its revolution. This is a fact worthy of note, since movement in a wheel is so much slower as it is nearer to the centre of the revolving object.

A wave of the sea always breaks in front of its base, and that portion of the crest will then be lower which before was highest.

Observe the motion of the surface of the water, how it resembles that of hair, which has two movements – one depends on the weight of the hair, the other on the direction of the curls; thus the water forms whirling eddies, one part following the impetus of the chief current, and the other following the incidental motion and return flow.

If a drop of water falls into the sea when it is calm, it must of necessity follow that the whole surface of the sea is raised imperceptibly, seeing that water cannot be compressed within itself like air.

The sun has never seen any shadow.

The colours in the middle of the rainbow mingle together. The bow in itself is not in the rain nor in the eye that sees it; though it is generated by the rain, the sun and the eye. The rainbow is always seen by the eye that is between the rain and

the body of the sun; hence if the sun is in the east and the rain is in the west it will appear on the rain in the west.

. . . The radiance of the sun or other luminous body remains in the eye for some time after it has been seen, and the motion of a single firebrand whirled rapidly in a circle causes this circle to seem one continuous uniform flame.

The drops of rain seem continuous threads descending from the clouds; and herein one may see how the eye preserves the impressions of moving things which it sees.

The birds which fly swiftly, keeping at the same distance above the ground, beat their wings downwards and behind them; downwards to the extent needed to prevent the bird from descending, backwards according as it wishes to advance with greater speed.

The speed of the bird is checked by the opening and spreading out of its tail.

In all the changes which birds make in their directions they spread out their tail.

dragonfly The pannicola flies with four wings, and when those in front are raised those behind are lowered.

But it is necessary for each pair to be sufficient of itself to sustain the whole weight.

When one pair is raised the other is lowered.

This is the reverse of the tongue, and its surface is rough in many animals and especially in the leonine species, such as lions, panthers, leopards, lynxes, cats and the like which have the surface of their tongues very rough as though covered with minute somewhat flexible nails; and when they lick their skin these nails penetrate to the root of the hairs, and act like combs in removing the small animals which feed on them.

And I once saw how a lamb was licked by a lion in our city of Florence, where there are always twenty-five to thirty of them, and they bear young. The lion with a few strokes of his tongue stripped off the whole fleece of the lamb, and after having made it bare, ate it.

The branches always start above the leaf.

A leaf always turns its upper side towards the sky so that it may the better be able to receive over its whole surface the dew

which drops gently from the atmosphere; and these leaves are
so distributed on the plants that one covers another as little as
possible, but they lie alternately one above another as is seen in
the ivy which covers the walls. And this alternation serves two
ends; that is in order to leave spaces so that the air and sun
may penetrate between them – and the second purpose of it is
that the drops which fall from the first leaf may fall onto the
fourth, or onto the sixth in the case of other trees.

Young plants have more transparent leaves and more lustrous
bark than old ones; and particularly the walnut is lighter
coloured in May than in September.

The rings on the cross-section of the branch of a tree show the
number of years, and the greater or smaller width of these rings
show which years were wetter and which drier. They also show
the direction in which the branch was turned, for the part that
was turned towards the north grows thicker than that turned
towards the south, so that the centre of the stem is nearer to the
bark that faces south than to that on the north side.

Translated from
the Italian by
Irma A. Richter
Leonardo Da Vinci

Although this is of no importance in painting I want nevertheless to describe it in order to leave out as little as possible of
what I know about trees.

Observation   Now and then concentrating
on the very small,

focusing my attention
on a very small area

like this crack in sandstone
perpetually wet with seepage,

getting so close
to moss, liverwort and fern

it becomes a forest
with wild beasts in it,

birds in the branches
and crickets piping,

cicadas shrilling.
Someone seeing me

staring so fixedly
at nothing

might be excused
for thinking me vague, abstracted,

lost in introspection.
No! I am awake, absorbed,

W. Hart-Smith   just looking in a different direction.

The Wildlife of New York City It was the quiet hour in the city, the interlude following the rush of quitting time when everyone seemed to pause to take a breath, and then, revitalized, charged into the next frantic activity of the city after dark. The sheer walls still radiated a warmth from the sun, which had disappeared behind the tallest buildings leaving only its rosy afterglow, and along the dark streets far below a few coloured lights began to glow. It was too dark now to make a good picture, Martin thought. He had been crouched with his camera on the window ledge for the past three hours waiting for something to happen. Now he moved to crawl back inside the window.

At that moment the peregrine falcon he had been watching launched from its perching ledge and dropped. Its sharply pointed wings thrust powerfully, and the bird dived like a falling bullet. Martin tried to swing his camera back into position, but it was impossible to find the hurtling bird in the viewfinder of the telephoto. He saw it, lost it, found it again and then it was too late.

An explosion of white feathers momentarily obscured his view and a dead pigeon spiralled downward. The peregrine flared up at the moment of contact, and the thump of the pigeon's body hitting the flat tarpaper roof sounded clearly from across the street. Now the falcon dropped leisurely to feast on its prey. Martin had missed the picture by a mile.

As if resigned to disappointment, Martin put his camera aside and watched the falcon drag the dead pigeon to the spot where it had chosen to dine. Near stumplike angles made by a group of ventilators, the falcon began to pluck feathers from its prey. Martin was not terribly upset at having missed the photograph. Similar, repeated failures had made him somewhat immune to the frustration of pictures seen and not taken.

The scene of a wild peregrine falcon at the moment of knocking a pigeon out of the sky over Manhattan Island was the shot Martin considered at the time as the most significant and graphic picture to illustrate the paradox of wild animals living in the seemingly unnatural environment of the great city. But really, Martin thought as he looked out from his place in the window, this was not an unlikely habitat for a falcon once the strangeness was put out of mind. The cliffs and canyons of the city made wind baffles to produce perfect flying air, differences in heat-radiating surfaces made for a great variety of updrafts and thermal air currents, and it seemed as if there were enough

pigeons along Fifth Avenue alone to feed all the falcons in the world.

He watched the falcon hold the prey down with its talons as it ripped off chunks of bloody meat. White feathers swirled around the rooftop. Caught in eddying air currents, the feathers spiralled slowly. Then they reached the canyon between two tall buildings and shot upward for a thousand feet in a fast-rising updraft. The editors had thought it unlikely he could find enough wildlife living in the city to have the story make a point. They would be surprised by this picture, Martin thought. He wanted to get some material in to the magazine as soon as possible. Maybe with something tangible to sell his idea, he could get an advance. He wished he had not missed the picture.

The bird gorged down a last morsel, carefully wiped its beak, and picked up a large chunk of meat. It flew with the meat in its talons, crossed the intersection of two of Manhattan's busiest streets, and landed on a huge rooftop billboard. Lights were already flashing on the sign, illuminating the awesomely vast bosom of a movie queen. She was painted in golden repose, a testimonial, Martin supposed, to the lung development one could expect from the featured brand of cigarette. From some-where up there in the cleavage he heard the greedy cries of fledgling peregrines. It was the same cry that came from windworn potholes in the ancient cliffs of western mountains. Dinner was served just the same in the city.

Martin turned away and gathered up his equipment. Then he took one more glance, as much at the unbelievable bosom, perhaps, as at the nesting site, and his eye caught an unusual movement. He squinted through the telephoto and focused carefully.

A human figure, a boy it appeared to be, was crawling along the topmost edge of the sign. A single ray of sun still angled between shafts of skyscrapers to the west and struck the sign like an orange-filtered spotlight. The figure would have been invisible from the street. So inconspicuous would it be, in fact, from any lower angle, that the boy must have been quite sure he was not observed. The two adult peregrines were now in the air above him. Their calls were shrill and they made quick steep dives at the intruder, their talons missing the boy's head only by inches. One well-delivered blow could easily have sent the boy tumbling to the sidewalk. The velocity of those short powerful stoops was remarkable. But the boy seemed completely oblivious to the birds hovering and squawking and diving like angry hornets above his head.

Martin's first impulse was to rush to the rooftop and call the boy away. He was as much concerned about the falcon's eggs or fledglings as he was for the lad's safety. Now that Martin had discovered the aerie, he did not wish to see the birds disturbed or driven from their nest. He thought of telephoning the fire department or the police, who would remove the boy for more humanitarian reasons than those which bothered Martin. But this would create so much activity and excitement that the birds would be even more upset. While these thoughts went through his mind, he continued to watch the strange performance through the magnification of his camera lens, and he realized that the lad had the situation very well in hand and that it was not his intention to disturb the nest.

nest of a bird of prey

The boy was now in a position directly over the spot where the bird with the meat had disappeared. He lay on the top of the sign and his head disappeared up to the shoulders. Apparently there was a hole up there where he could see down into the inner workings of the sign. Martin assumed that he was peering into the nest and judged his position to be only ten feet or so above where he thought the aerie was located. The pair of adult birds continued to harass him, now skimming close to his upturned rear. One of them made contact, and Martin saw the boy react by waving his hand impatiently at the bird as if to shoo it away.

At last he withdrew his head and began carefully to make his way backward along the sign in the direction from which he had come. The lens was opened to its fullest aperture, and Martin clicked the shutter as the boy was in perfect silhouette. Snapping the release was an almost automatic gesture. Martin was looking through the camera and when the boy was in a position to make the best composition, Martin merely pushed the button. He didn't think about it at the time. To him then, it was just a wasted exposure.

Then the sun dropped completely, quickly extinguishing the scene, just as the figure, now jet black against the lowering skyline, disappeared over the coping and onto the roof. . . .

It was no great naturalist's feat to discover much of the insect life of the city, and in little more than a week Martin recorded something of the life history of nearly a hundred forms of wildlife, all reproducing their kind and living out their lives within the shadows of the skyscrapers. On warm nights a great variety of moths, scarab beetles and other insects batted at the lights of certain buildings. Martin soon discovered that signs illuminated with lights of particular colours and those which were so displayed as to be seen from great distances apparently attracted specimens from miles away, but that some signs, no matter how prominently placed and brightly illuminated, were not enticing to the insects. Red neons were evidently not exciting. Blue-white lights, on the other hand, must drive certain night-flying insects into states of wild ecstasy, for at times their bodies frantically batted the hollow tubes of light in such numbers that a sound was produced like the roll of miniature drums, and the carcasses of spent insects littered the sidewalks each morning beneath the darkened silhouettes of the teasing bulbs like exhausted bodies left from a great bacchanal of the arthropods.

revelry

Martin found birds nesting everywhere in the city – sparrows, starlings and pigeons – under tiles, in the mouths of gargoyles, on building ledges, in a shoe hanging from its laces on a fire escape, even in an operating traffic light. And although he did not venture with his camera as far afield even as Central Park (where in the course of a year a bird-watcher could conceivably observe over two-hundred species of native-land birds) because he felt this more natural setting was not really a part of the strictly urban environment he had set out to illustrate, Martin was able to find seventeen varieties of birds inhabiting the concrete cliffs and asphalt meadows of the city itself.

The various species of gulls, ducks and shore birds that wander the rivers and waterways of the city provided him with shots of another ten kinds of birds, and a picture of a belted kingfisher perched on an abutment of George Washington Bridge high over the Hudson River and holding a killifish in its beak gave him a good double – two species, that is – in a single exposure.

Martin had always thought of pigeons as being strictly day-flying birds, and he was surprised to find them, in defiance of all ornithological rules, abroad after dark, swooping through the skies and pecking in the gutters of Times Square at midnight. The lights were ablaze, and flocks of pigeons sailed past in ceaseless waves, exploiting the handouts of late evening theatre-goers, walking the sidewalks, and winging in short bursts from one side of the street to the other. Their flights across the multicoloured neons and blinking bulbs made fascinating studies in abstraction for Martin's camera.

If Martin had wished to concentrate on the more civilized of nature's creatures within the city he would have emphasized the hosts of fleas, bedbugs, bookworms, clothes moths, silverfish, termites and cockroaches, the rats and mice, starlings and English sparrows that are so much a part of man's ultimate habitat that they are dependent upon it. But he did not want his city to seem populated predominantly with vermin. He filmed these animals, to be sure, as a vital and interesting part of this strange animal community. But he found the more respectable members of the environment, the ones perhaps not so long adapted, even more fascinating and possessed of considerably more charm. . . .

Archie paused watching two thin lines of ants going each way from a crack in the curb, across the sidewalk, to a cave under broken mortar between two bricks. . . .

Archie reached down toward the sidewalk. His extended finger paused over the columns, waiting for a space between the tightly crowded ants, then being very careful not to crush an insect, he drew his finger quickly along the cement, directly across the ant's invisible trail. Immediately the ants that came to the place where his finger had crossed became confused and greatly agitated. They blundered to right and left, working their feelers rapidly, apparently in a panic.

'I guess they follow a scent trail,' he said. 'The odour of my fingertip loused them up.'

Archie waited until the first ant had worked out the trail across the finger-wide void and the moving lines had resumed.

Then he stood up. . . .

Martin's work in the lot this morning was with the small creatures close to the soil, and his kit included a tripod, which he did not ordinarily use except for critically exacting work, and a bellows for his lenses which permitted him to get extremely close views of insects and spiders.

While Archie was prowling through a pile of old automobile parts, turning over rusted doors and fenders, Martin had discovered a battered engine crankcase which lay open like a dishpan beside the dismantled cylinder block. It was black with the caked grease of many years' use, and a kind of hard petroleum varnish coated the metal and made it invulnerable to the corrosive elements of nature. The walls were covered with brown plant-slime and vivid green hairs of algae lay like windblown grass on the surface of a hand's depth of trapped rainwater. Within the rusty shores of this small reservoir was a miniature community of pond life, complete and active in its own cycle of existence. Water boatmen and mosquito larvae rowed and wiggled through its depths, creatures small and unidentifiable without the aid of a magnifying lens squirmed in the algae, and a school of dark polliwogs sucked at the surface and dived with speedy flourishes as if they had some place to go.

tadpoles

Martin finished filming the pond and set up his equipment at the other end of the lot.

An hour later Archie had grown tired of watching Martin at his tedious manoeuvres to photograph a funnel-web spider devouring a fly within her nest in an empty plastic bottle, and he lay taking the sun, his face turned up to the sky.

'Look,' he said. 'Look up there.' He squinted through fingers laced across his eyes.

Martin stared for several moments before he spotted the object. It was a large soaring bird, a dot only, high above, most likely a red-tailed hawk, Archie said, cutting great loops across the sky.

'In spring and fall they pass over the city by the hundreds,' Archie said. 'I didn't know hawks migrated like that before we came here. Back home we never used to see flights of hawks like I do here. I've heard that one winter when it was real cold up in the north, snowy owls migrated clear down here and roosted on the buildings and in the trees in Central Park. And last winter I watched bald eagles perched on pads of ice and floating down the Hudson.'

The soaring hawk was now a speck as it sailed out toward the west. 'You wonder what he was doing flying around over the city,' Martin mused. 'It must look strange and foreboding to him from way up there.'

Archie didn't reply.

'I wonder how a hawk ever overcomes his fear,' Martin said.

'How he gets the courage to come down out of the sky and start knocking pigeons off the building ledges? Like the peregrine falcons? How does the first one, the first pair, begin? Do you realize,' he said, 'how frightening it all must seem to them?'

'I realize,' Archie said.

'They don't get trapped into it. There's plenty of wild country for them. It isn't as if they *have* to live in the city. I wonder if two animals of the same species, like our peregrine falcons, for example, one living in the native habitat, the other in the city, have great psychological differences?

'You think of city animals, and it's natural to think of corrupt, unhealthy, vermin types. That's just an idea, not necessarily true, a connotation you get from the rats and cockroaches. But I wonder if our peregrines are different in some way from the peregrines of the open countryside? In the wilderness animals seem to be at peace with their environment. I wonder if they are at peace here in the city – or are they somehow more savage?'

Martin's thoughts were interrupted by a sound out on the river. He and Archie both turned to look. Ripples showed on the river where a large fish had leaped, one of the few that still run through the gauntlet of pollution between the sea and the upper river. It rose once more and flopped back with a splash like a heavy log.

'Maybe the peregrines are like that old fish,' Martin said. 'Maybe this is simply their territory and they are only staying with it. Maybe they didn't come to the city at all, but are here merely because their ancestors occupied this land long ago. And each summer when a new generation was born, the ones that went away never came back, and the city grew up around the ones who stayed. I think that's probably what happened. I think the peregrines have just always been here.'

Archie began to walk. 'That's probably right. I can't imagine them choosing it. It's disappointing to think they'd choose to live here, feeding on stupid pigeons, which are so easy to catch, rather than having the satisfaction of a fat mallard at the end of a flashing chase. It's a big waste, a peregrine living here and getting fat on pigeons, when you think they are the fastest and most noble bird of prey in the world.'

Martin squinted through his viewfinder. This boy was getting to him somehow. Martin was not one to engage in such long-winded contemplations. He wondered what was happening to himself. The spider appeared in the magnification of his lens like an imaginary monster. The two bright eyes on the top of its head sparkled as if they had their own illumination, and the brown fangs below its palpi were gruesomely keen and sharp. The spider held its prey securely and the fly's last quiverings had ceased. Now the spider was sucking the insect's fluids. In a little while it would discard the dehydrated husk. With a flick of its forelegs it would toss the shell away from its web. Martin noticed the mound of dried insect carcasses where the wind had drifted them up against an old blue milk-of-magnesia bottle.

'There's an island,' Martin said, unable to cast off his reflective mood, 'in a great lake that was formed when the Panama Canal was built. There was a valley of lush jungle in central Panama which was occupied by multitudes of wildlife. When the canal was cut through, it flooded that valley and formed what is now called Gatun Lake.

'When they flooded the valley, every living creature was forced to higher ground. As the lake rose, the animals were crowded higher and higher onto the slopes of a mountain until they reached the very peak. The island which was formed is now called Barro Colorado. It is presently a biological research station, ideal for the purpose because all of the wildlife over a great many miles of jungle have been compressed onto this last remaining hill of dry land.

'Of course there were many hills that were completely submerged. Their occupants either swam on to higher islands or drowned.

'Our vacant lot, here, reminds me of one of those islands. The city has slowly risen up around it, compressing it, until this one spot with its fauna is all that remains. And this island, of course, is sinking just like one of those inundated islands in Gatun Lake – not sinking, really, but being overwhelmed just the same. It's only a matter of time.

'But the frightening thing is,' Martin continued, 'that with this inundation we have here, there may not be a Barro Colorado Island. It is as if this island we are now observing is behind a dam of limitless height. They keep building it higher, and the animals swim from one drowned island to the next higher one and then are driven off to seek another. And someday they will find they are on the highest mountain of all and the water is still rising.'

Martin didn't think Archie was listening; in fact he was talking as much to himself as he was to the boy. Martin looked up. As he suspected, Archie was walking slowly away along the shore with his hands in his pockets.

'Look here!' Archie's voice was unmistakably excited. Martin left his camera and walked over to where the boy was kneeling, looking down at the ground.

A mound of clean earth had been pushed up from beneath the surface trash. It lay dark and fertile, giving a hint at the subterranean purity of the soil. Somewhere in dark tunnels through the clean ground, a mole had encountered a stone. It had pushed the stone to the surface with its armloads of earth, a special stone for Archie to discover.

'It's an arrowhead!'

Without picking it up Archie cleared the earth away with his fingers from where the arrowhead lay. It was deeply side-notched, a classic point, perfectly chipped, the long flutes running in perfect symmetry from edge to centre. The material was red jasper with veins of blue and white, a stone which its ancient maker had picked for beauty as well as for utility.

'Beautiful!' Martin said.

Archie stared at the ground beneath his feet with thoughtful wonder. He looked up at the jagged line of buildings against the sky and back to the ancient artifact.

'An arrowhead here. I can't believe it.' He picked up the point, rubbed the dirt from its crevices, and polished it in his hand. 'Can you imagine a wilderness here? An Indian camp? A place where maybe deer came down to drink?' Archie's face was contorted with wonder and emotion. He put the arrowhead in his pocket. The point was there only a moment before he had to take it out and look at it again. Martin felt that this simple stone was the most treasured thing the boy had possessed in a long time.

'Yes,' Martin said. 'And all that was only six or eight generations ago. It doesn't seem like a very long time.'

Martin realized immediately that he had said the wrong thing. Archie looked across the river to where smoke from the factories was beginning to drift their way. The wind had changed. Overhead a big jet roared on its climb from Kennedy Airport. Archie's face grew sad.

'Do you think it will all be like this someday?'

The Concrete Wilderness
Jack Couffer

It was a question to which Martin did not reply, because he was afraid he knew the answer.

Glasgow and Salford In Glasgow, we lived at the toon-heid, a jungle of tenements as drab as prisons and warehouses as drab as tenements. But if Glasgow was a jungle, then Salford was a desert . . . a petrified desert of blackened and decayed brick; a city of cotton mills, coal-pits, factories and streets so alike that they might have been turned off a conveyor belt. Its bleakness was such as to cripple the imagination of any but the toughest kid. And black! Black as the Earl o' Hell's waistcoat!

Here lived spinners and weavers, back-tenters, little-piecers, bleachers, lathe-minders, machine-tool-makers, copper, brass and iron moulders, wood butchers, brickies, locomen, spidermen and coughing-johnnies from the asbestos mills.

Here, the kids practised finger-holds on the twenty-foot wall of the docks, collected spent cartridges from the fair on Spike Island, hunted for treasure on the Strawberry Hills' rubbish tip, and guided corrugated iron sleds down the clay slopes of the Mucky Mountains.

That was my city, my childhood world of streets full of the yells of playing kids. I grew up in those streets, sailed paper boats in the gutters, stalked Indians among the dustbins, raided neighbouring gangs for bonfire wood, and knew the first, sharp pangs of love.

I found my love on the gasworks croft,
Dreamed a dream by the old canal;
Kissed my girl by the factory wall,
Dirty Old Town, Dirty Old Town.

Heard a siren from the docks,
Saw a train set the night on fire,
Smelt the spring on the smoky wind,
Dirty Old Town, Dirty Old Town.

Every shadow was a hiding place for Red Indians, gangsters, gorillas and secret agents. Every lamp-post was a tree, a stake, a gallows. The distance between two sides of a street was a prairie, a jungle, a desert, an ocean, a deadly universe inhabited by hostile tribes and monsters with death-ray eyes. And the kids in the next street, and all the other streets . . . they were enemies, too . . . the pole gang, the square gang, the jumpers, the diehards, the peanut boys, the Percy Street boys . . . .

We are the boys of Percy Street,
We got big heads and we got big feet,
　　　Raid 'em!

We are the boys of Unwin Square,
Ride on the tram without any fare.
　　　Raid 'em!

We are the boys of Hanky Park,
Got cat's eyes, can see in the dark,
　　　Raid 'em!

You're all too dirty,
Dirty, dirty;
You're all too dirty,
I'll tell you.

You can't come into our street,
Our street, our street;
You can't come into our street
I'll tell you.

**Ewan MacColl
and Dominic Behan**

Car Fights Cat

In a London crescent curving vast
A cat sat –
Between two rows of molar houses
With birdsky in each grinning gap.

Cat small – coal and snow
Road wide – a zone of tar set hard and fast
With four-wheeled speedboats cutting
A dash
    for it from
             time to time.

King Cat walked warily midstream
As if silence were no warning on this silent road
Where even a man would certainly have crossed
With hands in pockets and been whistling.

The cat heard it, but royalty and indolence
Weighed its paws to hobnailed boots
Held it from the dragons-teeth of safety first and last,
Until some Daimler hurrying from work
Caused cat to stop and wonder where it came from –
Instead of zig-zag scattering to hide itself.

Maybe a deaf malevolence descended
And cat thought car would pass in front –
So spun and walked all fur and confidence
Into the dreadful tyre-treads . . . .
A wheel caught hold of it and
FEARSOME THUDS
Sounded from the night-time of black axles in
UNEQUAL FIGHT
That stopped the heart to hear it.

But cat shot out with limbs still solid,
Bolted – spitting fire and gravel
At unjust God who built such massive
Catproof motorcars in his graven image,
Its mind made up to lose and therefore win
By winging towards
The wisdom toothgaps of the canyon houses

Alan Sillitoe   LEGS AND BRAIN INTACT.

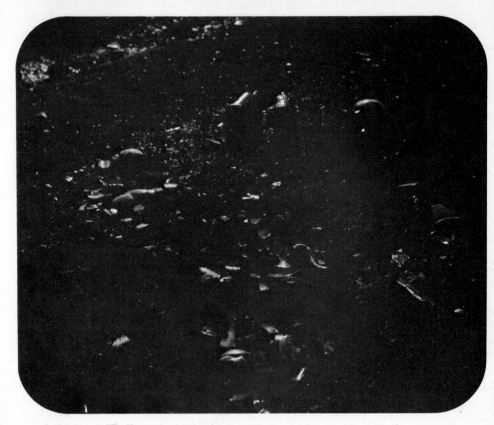

Between Walls   the back wings
of the

hospital where
nothing

will grow lie
cinders

in which shine
the broken

William Carlos   pieces of a green
Williams   bottle

The winter afternoon   The winter afternoon darkens.
The shoemaker bends close to the shoe,
his hammer raps faster.

An old woman waits,
Charles Reznikoff   rubbing the cold from her hands

Thames Scene

A zinc afternoon. The barges black,
And black the funnels of tugs nosing
Phlegm-coloured waves slap-slapping
Stone wharves. A smell of sacking
And soot. Grey chimneys, and statues

Alan Ross

Grey with cold, and grey lifebelts.

Hats   Hats, where do you belong?
                 what is under you?

           On the rim of a skyscraper's forehead
           I looked down and saw: hats: fifty thousand hats:
           Swarming with a noise of bees and sheep, cattle and waterfalls,
           Stopping with a silence of sea grass, a silence of prairie corn.

Carl Sandburg   Hats: tell me your high hopes.

People Who Must   I painted on the roof of a skyscraper.
I painted a long while and called it a day's work.
The people on a corner swarmed and the traffic cop's whistle
    never let up all afternoon.
They were the same as bugs, many bugs on their way –
Those people on the go or at a standstill;
And the traffic cop a spot of blue, a splinter of brass,
Where the black tides ran around him
And he kept the street. I painted a long while
Carl Sandburg   And called it a day's work.

41

Once at Piertarvit

Once at Piertarvit,
one day in April,
the edge of spring,
with the air a-ripple,
a sea like knitting,
as Avril and Ann
and Ian and I
walked in the wind
along the headland,
Ian threw an apple
high over Piertarvit.

Not a great throw,
you would say, if you saw it,
but good for Ian.
His body tautened,
his arm let go
like a flesh-and-bone bow,
and the hard brown apple
left over from autumn
flew up and up,
crossing our gaze,
from the cliff at Piertarvit.

Then, all at once, horror
glanced off our eyes,
Ann's, mine, Avril's.
As the apple curved
in the stippled sky,
at the top of its arc,
it suddenly struck
the shape of a bird –
a gull that had glided
down from nowhere
above Piertarvit.

We imagined the thud
and the thin ribs breaking,
blood, and the bird
hurtling downward.
No such thing.
The broad wings wavered
a moment only,
then air sustained them.
The gull glided on

while the apple fell
in the sea at Piertarvit.

Nobody laughed.
Nobody whistled.
In that one moment,
our world had faltered.
The four of us stood
stock-still with horror,
till, breaking the spell,
Ian walked away
with a whirl in his head.
The whole sky curdled
over Piertarvit.

I followed slowly,
with Ann and Avril
trailing behind.
We had lost our lightness.
Even today,
old as we are,
we would find it hard
to say, without wonder,
'Ian hit a bird
with an apple, in April,
once at Piertarvit.'

Alastair Reid

Lackaday   Today is not Sat or Sun or Mon or Tues
Or Wed or Thurs or Fri.
Today is Lackaday.
How did you sleep? Fair.
How do you feel? About the same.
What's new? Not much.
What do you know? Not a thing.
What'll you have? The usual.
What'll it be? The same all around.
Who did you see? The same old bunch.
What do you feel like doing? Anything you say.
Don't you think so? Sure do.
Wasn't he? Sure was.
Wasn't she? You bet.
Well. . . . Well. . . .

Robert Paul Smith   Today is Lackaday.

Sunday Afternoons

On Sunday afternoons
In winter, snow in the air,
People sit thick as birds
In the station buffet-bar.
They know one another.
Some exchange a few words
But mostly they sit and stare
At the urns and the rock buns.

Not many trains today.
Not many are waiting for trains
Or waiting for anything
Except for the time to pass.
The fug is thick on the glass
Beyond which, through honks and puffing,
An express shrugs and strains
To sidings not far away.

Here no one is saying good-bye:
Tears, promises to write,
Journeys, are not for them.
Here there are other things
To mull over, till the dark brings
Its usual burdensome
Thoughts of a place for the night,
A bit of warm and dry.

On Sunday afternoons
The loudspeaker has little to say
Of wherever the few trains go.
Not many are travellers.
But few are as still as these
Who sit here out of the snow,
Passing the time away
Till the night begins.

Anthony Thwaite

Lazying Downriver   Two or three days and nights went by; I reckon I might say they swum by, they slid along so quiet and smooth and lovely. Here is the way we put in the time. It was a monstrous big river down there – sometimes a mile and a half wide; we run nights, and laid up and hid daytimes; soon as night was most gone we stopped navigating and tied up – nearly always in the dead water under a towhead; and then cut young cottonwoods and willows, and hid the raft with them. Then we set out the lines. Next we slid into the river and had a swim, so as to freshen up and cool off; then we set down on the sandy bottom where the water was about knee deep, and watched the daylight come. Not a sound anywheres – perfectly still – just like the whole world was asleep, only sometimes the bullfrogs a-cluttering, maybe. The first thing to see, looking away over the water, was a kind of dull line – that was the woods on t'other side; you couldn't make nothing else out; then a pale place in the sky; then more paleness spreading around; then the river softened up away off, and warn't black any more, but grey; you could see little dark spots drifting along ever so far away – punts trading scows, and such things; and long black streaks – rafts; sometimes you could hear a sweep screaking; or jumbled-up voices, it was still, and sounds come so far; and by-and-by you could see a streak on the water which you know by the look of the streak that there's a snag there in a swift current which breaks on it and makes the streak look that way; and you see the mist curl up off the water, and the east reddens up, and the river, and you make out a log cabin, in the edge of the woods, away on the bank on t'other side of the river, being a woodyard, likely, and piled by them cheats so you can throw a dog through it anywheres; then the nice breeze springs up, and comes fanning you from over there, so cool and fresh and sweet to smell on account of the woods and the flowers; but sometimes fish like pike not that way, because they've left dead fish laying around, gars and such, and they do get pretty rank; and next you've got the full day, and everything smiling in the sun, and the song-birds just going it!

A little smoke couldn't be noticed now, so we would take some fish off the lines and cook up a hot breakfast. And afterwards we would watch the lonesomeness of the river, and kind of lazy along, and by and by lazy off to sleep. Wake up by and by, and look to see what done it, and maybe see a steamboat coughing along upstream, so far off towards the other side you couldn't tell nothing about her only whether she was a stern-wheel or side-wheel; then for about an hour there wouldn't be nothing to hear nor nothing to see – just solid lonesomeness. Next you'd see a raft sliding by, away off yonder, and maybe a clot galoot on it chopping, because they're most always doing it on a raft; you'd see the axe flash and come down – you don't hear nothing; you see that axe go up again, and by the time it's above the man's head then you hear the *k'chunk*! – it had took *Huckleberry Finn* all that time to come over the water. So we would put in the **Mark Twain** day, lazying around, listening to the stillness.

Wonder Wander   in the afternoon the children walk like ducks
like geese
like from here to there
eyeing bird-trees puppy dogs candy windows
sun balls ice cream wagons
lady bugs rose bushes fenced yards vacant lots
tall buildings
and other things
big business men take big business walks
wear big business clothes
carry big business briefcases   talk about
big business affairs in
big business voices
young girls walk pretty on the streets
stroll the avenues linger by
shop windows   wedding rings   lady hats
shiny dresses   fancy shoes
whisper like turkey hens   passing the time
young men stride on parade   dream headed
wild eyed   eating up the world
with deep glances   rubbing empty fingers
in the empty pockets and
planning
me, I wander around soft-shoed   easy-legged
watching the scene as it goes
finding things   sea-gull feathers   pink baby roses
everytime I see a letter on the sidewalk
I stop and look   it might be
Lenore Kandel   for me

A Sunny Day The curved leaves of the little tree are shining;
the bushes across the street are purple with flowers.
A man with a red beard talks to a woman with yellow hair;
she laughs like the clash of brass cymbals.

Two negresses are coming down the street;
they munch lettuce
and pull the leaves slowly out of a bag.

The pigeons wheel in the bright air,
now white, now the grey backs showing.
They settle down upon a roof;
the children shout, the owner swings his bamboo.

The sun shone into the bare, wet tree;
it became a pyramid of criss-cross lights,
and in each corner the light nested.

These days the papers in the street
leap into the air or burst across the lawns –
not a scrap but has the breath of life:
these in a gust of wind
play about,

Charles Reznikoff those for a moment lie still and sun themselves.

The Beach The beach is a quarter of golden fruit,
a soft ripe melon
sliced to a half-moon curve,
having a thick green rind
of jungle growth;
and the sea devours it
with its sharp,

W. Hart-Smith white teeth.

Waking from a Sounds like big
Nap on the Beach rashers of bacon frying.
I look up from where I'm lying
expecting to see stripes

red and white. My eyes drop shut,
stunned by the sun.
Now the foam is flame, the long
troughs charcoal, but

still it chuckles and sizzles, it
burns and burns, and never gets done.
The sea is that

May Swenson fat.

Cornish Coast

Here the winds are so black and terrible. They rush with such force that the house shudders, though the old walls are very solid and thick. Only occasionally the gulls rise very slowly into the air. And all the while the wind rushes and thuds and booms, and all the while the sea is hoarse and heavy. It is strange, one forgets the rest of life. It shuts one in within its massive violent world. Sometimes a wave bursts with a great explosion against one of the outlying rocks, and there is a tremendous ghost standing high on the sea, a great tall whiteness.

D. H. Lawrence

The Winds

flowing edge to edge
their clear edges meeting –
the winds of this northern March –
blow the bark from the trees
the soil from the field
the hair from the heads of
girls, the shirts from the backs
of the men, roofs from the
houses, the cross from the
church, clouds from the sky
the fur from the faces of
wild animals, crusts
from scabby eyes, scales from
the mind and husbands from wives

William Carlos Williams

Rare Weather

In a really dry desert country
A drop of rainwater hit a man, and he was so surprised they had to throw two buckets of dirt over his face to bring him to.

In windy country
We keep track of the wind by hanging a log chain on a post. If it stands out straight, there's a breeze, but when it gets to whipping around, and links snap off, look out; it's likely to be windy by sundown!

Thirsty work
A farmer, leaving the arid south-west: asked why he was leaving: 'I'm tired of sweating dust, that's why. Out here the only rains are dust storms. Buzzards have to wear goggles and fly backwards to keep from choking to death, and grasshoppers carry haversacks to keep from starving. My mouth is always so dry the only way I can whistle to my dog is by ringing a bell.'

In wet country
'Even the pores of my hide are sprouting watercress . . . the chicken grow web-footed and their eggs hatch out turtles. . . .'

Traditional American

Seasons

Spring:	Slippy, drippy, nippy.
Summer:	Showery, flowery, bowery.
Autumn:	Hoppy, croppy, poppy.
Winter:	Wheezy, sneezy, breezy.

Sydney Smith

The Rain in Spain   Unmediterranean
today, the punctual sun
sulks and stays in

and heavily down the mountain
across olive and pine
rolls a scrim of rain.

Faces press to windows.
Strangers moon and booze.
Innkeepers doze.

Slow lopsided clocks
tick away weeks.
Rudely the weather knocks

and starts up old ills,
insect-itch, boils.
The mail brings bills.

Lovers in their houses
quarrel and make promises
or, restless, dream of cities.

Ghosts in the rafters mutter.
Goats thump and clatter.
Birds augur water.

The Dutch poet is sick.
The postman kicks his dog.
Death overtakes a pig.

Books turn sudden-sour.
Thunder grumbles somewhere.
Sleepers groan in nightmare,

each sure that the sky teems
with his personal phantoms,
each doomed to his own bad dreams.

For who is weather-wise
enough to recognize
Alastair Reid   which ills are the day's, which his?

Summer Storm The heat was intense that week, and in church on Sunday morning Laura gasped for air. Shimmering heat waves quivered upward outside the windows, and the fitful little breezes were hot.

When church was over, Almanzo was waiting outside to take Laura home. As he helped her into the buggy he said, 'Your mother asked me to dinner, and afterward we will exercise these horses again. It will be hot this afternoon,' he said in the buggy, 'but driving will be pleasanter than sitting in the house, if it doesn't storm.'

'My feathers are sewed on tight,' Laura laughed. 'So let the wind blow.'

Soon after Ma's good Sunday dinner, they set out, driving southward over the gently rolling, endless prairie. The sun shone fiercely, and even in the shade of the swiftly moving buggy top, the heat was oppressive. Instead of flowing smoothly and cool, the breeze came in warm puffs.

The shimmering heat-waves made a silvery appearance that retreated before them on the road ahead, like water, and phantom winds played in the grasses, twisting them in frantic writhings and passing on, up and away.

After a time, dark clouds began to gather in the north-west, and the heat grew still more intense.

'This is a queer afternoon. I think we'd better go home,' Almanzo said.

'Yes, let's do, and hurry,' Laura urged. 'I don't like the way the weather feels.'

The black mass of clouds was rising quickly as Almanzo turned the horses toward home. He stopped them and gave the reins to Laura. 'Hold them while I put on the buggy curtains. It's going to rain,' he said.

Quickly, behind the buggy, he unbuttoned the straps that held the top's back curtain rolled up. He let it unroll, and buttoned it at the sides and bottom, tightly closing in the back of the buggy. Then from under the seat he brought out the two side curtains, and buttoned them along their tops and sides to the sides of the buggy top, closing them in.

Then, back in his seat, he unrolled the rubber storm apron, and set the pleat in its bottom edge over the top of the dashboard, where it fitted snugly.

Laura admired the cleverness of this storm apron. There was a slot in it that fitted over the whipsocket, so the whip stood up in its place. There was a slit, through which Almanzo passed the lines; he could hold them in his hands under the storm apron, and a flap fell over the slit, to keep rain from coming in. The apron was so wide that it came down to the buggy box on either side, and it buttoned up to the side frames of the buggy top.

All this was done quickly. In a moment or two, Laura and Almanzo were snugly sheltered in a box of rubber curtains. No rain could come through the apron, the curtains nor the buggy top overhead. Above the edge of the storm apron, that was as high as their chins, they could look out.

As Almanzo took the lines from Laura and started the horses, he said, 'Now let it rain!'

'Yes,' Laura said, 'if it must, but maybe we can beat the storm home.'

Almanzo was already urging the team. They went swiftly, but even more swiftly the black cloud rose, rolling and rumbling in the sky. Laura and Almanzo watched it in silence. The whole earth seemed silent and motionless in terror. The sound of the horses' fast-trotting feet and the tiny creaks of the speeding buggy seemed small in the stillness.

The swelling great mass of clouds writhed and wrestled, twisting together as if in fury and agony. Flickers of red lightning stabbed through them. Still the air was motionless fringe and there was no sound. The heat increased. Laura's bangs were damp with perspiration, and uncurled on her forehead, while trickles ran down her cheeks and her neck. Almanzo urged on the horses.

Almost overhead now, the tumbling, swirling clouds changed from black to a terrifying greenish-purple. They seemed to draw themselves together, then a groping finger slowly came out of them and stretched down, trying to reach the earth. It reached, and pulled itself up, and reached again.

'How far away is that?' Laura asked.

'Ten miles, I'd say,' Almanzo replied.

It was coming toward them, from the north-west, as they sped toward the north-east. No horses, however fast they ran, could outrun the speed of those clouds. Green-purple, they rolled in the sky above the helpless prairie, and reached toward it playfully as a cat's paw torments a mouse.

A second point came groping down, behind the first. Then another. All three reached and withdrew and reached again, down from the writhing clouds.

Then they all turned a little toward the south. One after another, quickly, all three points touched the earth, under the cloud-mass and travelling swiftly with it. They passed behind the buggy, to the west, and went on southward. A terrific wind blew suddenly, so strong that the buggy swayed, but that storm had passed. Laura drew a long, shaking breath.

'If we had been home, Pa would have sent us down cellar,' she said. 'And I would have been glad to go,' she added.

'We'd have needed a cellar, if that storm had come our way. I never did run to a cyclone cellar, but if I ever meet a cloud like that, I will,' Almanzo admitted.

The wind abruptly changed. It blew from the south-west and brought a sudden cold with it.

'Hail,' Almanzo said.

'Yes,' said Laura. Somewhere, hail had fallen from that cloud.

Everyone at home was glad to see them. Laura had never seen Ma so pale, nor so thankful. Pa said that they had shown good judgement in turning back when they did. 'That storm is doing bad damage,' he said.

'It's a good idea, out here in this country, to have a cellar,' said Almanzo. He asked what Pa thought of their driving out across country, where the storm had passed, to see if anyone needed help. So Laura was left at home, while Pa and Almanzo drove away.

Though the storm was gone and the sky now clear, still they were nervous.

The afternoon passed, and Laura had changed into her weekday clothes and with Carrie's help had done the chores, before Pa and Almanzo came back. Ma set a cold supper on the table, and while they ate they told what they had seen in the path of the storm.

One settler not far south of town had just finished threshing his wheat crop from a hundred acres. It had been a splendid crop, that would have paid all his debts and left money in the bank. He and the threshers had been working that day to finish the job, and he was on a strawstack when they saw the storm coming.

He had just sent his two young boys to return a wagon he had borrowed from a neighbour to help in the threshing. He got into his cyclone cellar just in time. The storm carried away his grain, strawstacks and machinery, wagons, stables and house; everything. Nothing was left but his bare claim.

The two boys on the mules had disappeared completely. But just before Pa and Almanzo reached the place, the older boy had come back, stark naked. He was nine years old. He said that he and his brother were riding the mules home, running, when the storm struck them. It lifted them all together and carried them around in a circle, in the air, still harnessed together side by side. They were whirled around, faster and faster and higher, until he began to get dizzy and he shouted to his little brother to hold on tight to his mule. Just then the air filled thickly with whirling straw and darkened so that he could see nothing. He felt a jerk of the harness breaking apart, and then he must have fainted. For the next thing he knew, he was alone in clear air.

He could see the ground beneath him. He was being carried around in a circle, all the time sinking a little, until finally he was not far above the earth. He tried to spring up, to get his feet under him, then struck the ground running, ran a little way, and fell. After lying there a few moments to rest, he got up and made his way home.

He had come to the ground a little more than a mile from his father's claim. There was not a shred of clothing left on him; even his high, laced boots had disappeared, but he was not hurt at all. It was a mystery how his boots had been taken from his feet without so much as bruising them.

Neighbours were searching far and wide for the other boy and the mules, but not a trace could be found of them. There could be hardly a hope that they were alive.

'Still, if that door came through,' Almanzo said.

'What door?' Carrie wanted to know.

That was the strangest thing that Pa and Almanzo had seen that day. It happened at another settler's claim, farther south. Everything had been stripped clean off his place, too. When this man and his family came up from their cyclone cellar, two bare spots were all that were left of stable and house. Oxen, wagon, tools, chickens, everything was gone. They had nothing but the clothes they wore, and one quilt that his wife had snatched to wrap around the baby in the cellar.

This man said to Pa, 'I'm a lucky man; I didn't have a crop to lose.' They had moved onto their claim only that spring, and he had been able to put in only a few sod potatoes.

That afternoon about sunset, as Pa and Almanzo were coming back from searching for the lost boy, they came by this place and stopped for a moment. The homesteader and his family had been gathering boards and bits of lumber that the storm had dropped, and he was figuring how much more he would have to get to build them some kind of shelter.

While they stood considering this, one of the children noticed a small dark object high in the clear sky overhead. It did not look like a bird, but it appeared to be growing larger. They all watched it. For some time it fell slowly toward them, and they saw that it was a door. It came gently down before them. It was the front door of this man's vanished claim shanty.

It was in perfect condition, not injured at all, not even scratched. The wonder was, where it had been all those hours, and that it had come slowly down from a clear sky, directly over the place where the claim shanty had been.

'I never saw a man more chirked up than he was,' said Pa.

'Now he doesn't have to buy a door for his new shanty. It even came back with the hinges on it.'

They were all amazed. In all their lives, none of them had ever heard of a stranger thing than the return of that door. It was awesome to think how far or how high it must have gone in air during all those hours.

'It's a queer country out here,' Pa said. 'Strange things happen.'

'Yes,' said Ma. 'I'm thankful that so far they don't happen to us.'

That next week Pa heard in town that the bodies of the lost boy and the mules had been found the next day. Every bone in them was broken. The clothing had been stripped from the boy and the harness from the mules. No scrap of clothing or harness was ever found.

These Happy Golden Years
Laura Ingalls Wilder

'Oh, they're wicked things'

We spend the night in a state park in O'Fallon, about twenty-five miles west of Saint Louis. The park is run by a friendly man named Jack Williams, who is glad of company this early in the camping season and spends the hour before sunset sitting on a hillside with us, doing most of the talking – a really remarkable feat, considering the kind of dust storm we can raise. It is pleasant to sprawl out in the grass, watching the sky turn pink and green, and listen to Jack Williams talking easily. He points out several oddly twisted and broken trees and says, 'A hurricane did that, two years back. Crumpled those trees just as easy as mashing potatoes. There wasn't a thing I could do about it.'

He sounds sad and a little guilty, as though even now he privately believes there must have been something he could have done to save the trees. Phil says, 'We just missed a twister around Indianapolis.' A newspaper had predicted that a Kansas hurricane would pass over the city the evening we were there, but it didn't. I chant, 'We just caught the fringes of it.' We have silently decided that the rainstorm we ran into that day was a fringe. The story will become true in time.

'Oh, they're wicked things,' Jack Williams says. 'We get small ones every couple of years, and there was one real big one come along seven years ago, the year they opened this park. Tore the whole house right off one fella, like a little wind takes off your hat, you know. Left him and his whole family huddling round the piano, hanging on to keep from taking off themselves. That's about the only things hurricanes won't take and blow somewheres else, pianos. I had a big brood mare once, solid, heavy, determined old girl, and she disappeared in one of those hurricanes, vanished right out of a pasture with a six-foot bob-wire fence around it. You know, she turned up two days later and two more bob-wire fences away, eating grass, calm as could be. No, I tell you, the only safe thing in a hurricane is a piano. Only thing *I* know of.'

Peter Beagle

WHEN A HURRICANE THREATENS

KEEP YOUR RADIO OR TV ON...AND LISTEN TO LATEST WEATHER BUREAU ADVICE TO SAVE YOUR *LIFE* AND POSSESSIONS

BEFORE THE WIND AND FLOOD

 HAVE GAS TANK FILLED... CHECK BATTERY AND TIRES.

HAVE SUPPLY OF DRINKING WATER. STOCK UP ON FOODS THAT NEED NO COOKING OR REFRIGERATION.

 HAVE ON HAND FLASHLIGHT, FIRST AID KIT, FIRE EXTINGUISHER, BATTERY-POWERED RADIO.

 STORE ALL LOOSE OBJECTS: TOYS, TOOLS, TRASH CANS, AWNINGS, ETC. BOARD OR TAPE UP ALL WINDOWS.

 GET AWAY FROM LOW AREAS THAT MAY BE SWEPT BY STORM TIDES OR FLOODS.

DURING THE STORM

STAY INDOORS... DON'T BE FOOLED IF THE CALM "EYE" PASSES DIRECTLY OVER... AND DON'T BE CAUGHT IN THE OPEN WHEN THE HURRICANE WINDS RESUME FROM THE *OPPOSITE* DIRECTION.

LISTEN TO YOUR RADIO OR TV FOR INFORMATION FROM THE WEATHER BUREAU, CIVIL DEFENSE, RED CROSS, AND OTHER AUTHORITIES.

AFTER THE STORM HAS PASSED

DO NOT DRIVE UNLESS NECESSARY. WATCH OUT FOR UNDERMINED PAVEMENT AND BROKEN POWER LINES.

REPORT DOWNED POWER WIRES, BROKEN WATER OR SEWER PIPES TO PROPER AUTHORITIES OR NEAREST POLICEMAN.

USE EXTREME CAUTION TO PREVENT OUTBREAK OF FIRE, OR INJURIES FROM FALLING OBJECTS.

USE PHONE FOR EMERGENCIES ONLY. JAMMED SWITCHBOARDS PREVENT EMERGENCY CALLS FROM GOING THROUGH.

YOUR ABILITY TO MEET EMERGENCIES WILL INSPIRE AND HELP OTHERS

U.S. DEPARTMENT OF COMMERCE • WEATHER BUREAU

The Hell of a Hurricane

'Sorry there is no return envelope,' wrote Linda Sage when she sent this report. 'Our post office has been blown away.'

At about 4 a.m. Martin and I woke up with the feeling that something was wrong. 'Let's see where the hurricane is,' he suggested, so we got out our tracking chart and turned on the radio. Sure enough, the capricious Celia had changed course. When we had gone to bed, she was heading for Houston, about two hundred miles up the coast. Now she was making a beeline for our backyard.

'Let's go!' I decided, scooping up a suitcase with one hand and plucking our baby out of his cot with the other. Martin took one last look at his new hi-fi equipment and I gazed fondly on our Conran curtains. Then we were charging through the night in our tiny Volkswagen, our baby asleep in the back and our cat curled up on the floor. Even now lightning was on every horizon and the wind was doing some preliminary exercises. Oh, to be back in England. . . .

Fifty miles inland we came across a small town on fairly high ground, which seemed a good place to ride out the storm. The rest of the day we sat in the safety of a motel room, with our ears glued to the radio as the hurricane spun its way to the central Texas coast. At 3 p.m. it struck land at Port Aransas and Aransas Pass, one the site of Martin's laboratory and the other of our home. Were we to be made jobless and homeless at the same time?

During the hurricane, residents who had been too stubborn to leave their houses were blasted with winds of 160 m.p.h. from the south-east. Then came the eye, bringing uncanny calm and time to look out at the chaos all around. Then the wind started up from the other direction, this time doing even more damage than before.

Shortly after the storm began, the radio and television stations from the Corpus Christi area were all silenced. 'The whole building is shaking, huge pieces of metal are flying around outside, the street is being lacerated by a hail of fine glass from broken windows, palm trees are bending into a U-shape. . . .' and then we heard no more. The television studio itself had been wrecked.

Soon all the telephone lines were dead too. The hurricane area was completely cut off from the outside world. Later that night, the small hospital in our home town managed to get out a message. Only its shell was left and it was housing hurricane victims urgently in need of blood, splints and medicines. Could anyone help?

When light broke the next day, the vast extent of the damage became visible. Corpus Christi, a city of 200,000, had few windows intact. The neighbouring towns of Rockport, Gregory and Portland were badly damaged. Ingleside was on fire from three huge oil storage tanks ignited by sparks from flying metal or lightning. But our home town, Aransas Pass, was worst hit of all. When we heard that 90 per cent of the buildings (most of which were made of wood, not brick) had been destroyed, we resigned ourselves. The longer we took, the longer we could hope. Part of the low-lying road had been washed away but we managed to negotiate it. As we neared home, the road was littered with torn-down cables, poles, rotting vegetation, and, at one point, a whole house which had been lifted up by the wind and deposited half way across the road. The fields, which stretch as far as the eye can see, had been laden with maize and cotton, ready for harvesting. Now the plants were bowed down on the ground, acknowledging an awesome force which had just passed their way.

Our hearts sank as we turned the corner of our road. But there was our house, four walls and a roof, all intact. But the sturdy, old oak trees surrounding it had been snapped in two like matchsticks and it was no longer surrounded by a fence. Hoof marks in the front garden told of stampeding cows seeking refuge from the storm. And the whole area looked as if winter had suddenly come – there was not a single leaf left on any of the trees.

Looking around now, we realize how lucky we were. We are surrounded by houses whose roofs have been snatched by the hurricane, piles of rubble that were once homes, mobile homes that were tossed up in the air and flung down again upside down, their bellies split open and their innards spilling out.

Cars are buried under piles of rubble, lorries are wrapped round trees, street signs scattered like confetti, and porches peeled off. Glass, metal, trees, dustbins clutter the streets. Shrimp boats are herded together in the harbour like sardines. Smaller boats look as if they were made of balsa wood. Silos resemble crushed aluminium tubes. Over the whole town hangs black, oily smoke and a smell of rotting debris. Last week there was a town here. Now there is a pile of refuse.

Like us, the rest of the town is back to pick up the pieces. A man stands in the remains of his house. 'That used to be the kitchen,' he says. A woman delves into the deep pile of objects heaped on the flattened walls of her house. She picks out a blouse and hangs it on a tree, smoothing out the folds. A family sits around its dining table, eating a midday meal from a tin, but they have no walls around them. Everywhere is the sound of sawing, hammering, screwing.

Our grocer waves and smiles from what used to be his shop. He wades his way out through crushed tins and broken glass. 'Guess I won't be open today.'

Linda Sage

The Forgotten City

When with my mother I was coming down
from the country the day of the hurricane,
trees were across the road and small branches
kept rattling on the roof of the car.
There was ten feet or more of water
making the parkways impassable with wind
bringing more rain in sheets. Brown torrents
gushed up through new sluices in the
valley floor so that I had to take what road
I could find bearing to the south and west,
to get back to the city. I passed through
extraordinary places, as vivid as any
I ever saw where the storm had broken
the barrier and let through
a strange commonplace: Long, deserted avenues
with unrecognized names at the corners and
drunken looking people with completely
foreign manners. Monuments, institutions
and in one place a large body of water
startled me with an acre or more of hot
jets spouting up symmetrically over it. Parks.
I had no idea where I was and promised myself
I would someday go back to study this
curious and industrious people who lived
in these apartments, at these sharp
corners and turns of intersecting avenues
with so little apparent communication
with an outside world. How did they get
cut off this way from representation in our
newspapers and other means of publicity
when so near the metropolis, so closely
surrounded by the familiar and the famous?

William Carlos Williams

Earthquake　　An old man's flamingo-coloured kite
Twitches higher over tiled roofs.
Idly gazing through the metal gauze
That nets the winter sun beyond my sliding windows,
I notice that all the telegraph poles along the lane
Are waggling convulsively, and the wires
Bounce like skipping-ropes round flustered birds.
The earth creeps under the floor. A cherry tree
Agitates itself outside, but it is no wind
That makes the long bamboo palisade
Begin to undulate down all its length.

The clock stammers and stops. There is a queer racket,
Like someone rapping on the wooden walls,
Then through the ceiling's falling flakes I see
The brass handles on a high chest of drawers
Dithering and dancing in a brisk distraction.
The lamp swings like a headache, and the whole house
Rotates slightly on grinding rollers.
Smoothly, like a spoilt child putting out a tongue,
A drawer shoots half-out, and quietly glides back again,
Closed with a snap of teeth, a sharper click
Than such a casual grimace prepared me for.

The stove-pipe's awkward elbow
Twangles its three supporting wires. Doors
Slam, fly open: my quiet maid erupts from
Nowhere, blushing furiously, yet smiling wildly
As if to explain, excuse, console and warn.
Together, like lost children in a fairy-tale
Who escape from an enchanter's evil cottage,
We rush out into the slightly unbalanced garden. A pole
Vibrates still like a plucked bass string,
But the ground no longer squirms beneath our feet,
And the trees are composing themselves, have birds again.

In the spooky quiet, a plane drones
Like a metal top, and though the sound
Gives a sense of disaster averted,
And is even oddly re-assuring, as
The pulse of confident engines,
Throbbing high above an electric storm, can comfort,
We feel that somewhere out of sight
Something has done its worst. Meanwhile,
The house tries to look as if nothing had happened,
And over the roof's subtle curves
Lets the flamingo-coloured kite fly undisturbed.

　　James Kirkup

Snow   The eye marvels at the beauty of its whiteness,
                   and the mind is amazed at its falling.
             He pours the hoarfrost upon the earth like salt,
                   and when it freezes, it becomes pointed thorns.
             The cold north wind blows,
                   and ice freezes over the water;
             it rests upon every pool of water,
The Bible   and the water puts it on like a breastplate.

The Coming of   The ribs of leaves lie in the dust,
the Cold   The beak of frost has pecked the bough,
                     The briar bears its thorn, and drought
                     Has left its ravage on the field.
                     The season's wreckage lies about,
                     Late autumn fruit is rotted now.
                     All shade is lean, the antic branch
                     Jerks skyward at the touch of wind,
                     Dense trees no longer hold the light,
                     The hedge and orchard grove are thinned.
                     The dank bark dries beneath the sun,
                     The last of harvesting is done.

All things are brought to barn and fold.
The oak leaves strain to be unbound,
The sky turns dark, the year grows old,
The buds draw in before the cold.

The small brook dies within its bed;
The stem that holds the bee is prone;
Old hedgerows keep the leaves; the phlox,
That late autumnal bloom is dead.

All summer green is now undone:
The hills are grey, the trees are bare,
The mould upon the branch is dry,
The fields are harsh and bare, the rocks
Gleam sharply on the narrow sight.
The land is desolate, the sun
No longer gilds the scene at noon;
Winds gather in the north and blow
Bleak clouds across the heavy sky,
And frost is marrow-cold, and soon
Theodore Roethke Winds bring a fine and bitter snow.

In the black season In the black season of deep winter
a storm of waves is roused
along the expanse of the world.
Sad are the birds of every meadow-plain
(except the ravens which feed on crimson blood)
at the clamour of fierce winter;
it is rough, black, dark, misty.
Dogs are vicious in cracking bones;
the iron pot is put on the fire
Anonymous after the dark black day.

To Build a Fire   Day had broken cold and grey, exceedingly cold and grey, when the man turned aside from the main Yukon trail and climbed the high earth-bank, where a dim and little-travelled trail led eastward through the fat spruce timberland. It was a steep bank, and he paused for breath at the top, excusing the act to himself by looking at his watch. It was nine o'clock. There was no sun nor hint of sun, though there was not a cloud in the sky. It was a clear day, and yet there seemed an intangible pall over the face of things, a subtle gloom that made the day dark, and that was due to the absence of sun. This fact did not worry the man. He was used to the lack of sun. It had been days since he had seen the sun, and he knew that a few more days must pass before that cheerful orb, due south, would just peep above the skyline and dip immediately from view.

The man flung a look back along the way he had come. The Yukon lay a mile wide and hidden under three feet of ice. On top of this ice were as many feet of snow. It was all pure white, rolling in gentle undulations where the ice jams of the freeze-up had formed. North and south, as far as his eye could see, it was unbroken white, save for a dark hairline that curved and twisted from around the spruce-covered island to the south, and that curved and twisted away into the north, where it disappeared behind another spruce-covered island. This dark hairline was the trail – the main trail – that led south five hundred miles to the Chilcoot Pass, Dyea and salt water; and that led north seventy miles to Dawson, and still on to the north a thousand miles to Nulato, and finally to St Michael, on Bering Sea, a thousand miles and half a thousand more.

But all this – the mysterious, far-reaching hairline trail, the absence of sun from the sky, the tremendous cold, and the strangeness and weirdness of it all – made no impression on the man. It was not because he was long used to it. He was a newcomer in the land, a *chechaquo*, and this was his first winter. The trouble with him was that he was without imagination. He was quick and alert in the things of life, but only in the things, and not in the significances. Fifty degrees below zero meant eighty-odd degrees of frost. Such fact impressed him as being cold and uncomfortable, and that was all. . . . Fifty degrees below zero stood for a bite of frost that hurt and that must be guarded against by the use of mittens, ear flaps, warm moccasins and thick socks. Fifty degrees below zero. That there should be anything more to it than that was a thought that never entered his head.

As he turned to go on, he spat speculatively. There was a sharp explosive crackle that startled him. He spat again. And again, in the air, before it could fall to the snow, the spittle crackled. He knew that at fifty below spittle crackled on the snow, but this spittle had crackled in the air. Undoubtedly it was colder than fifty below – how much colder he did not know. But the temperature did not matter. He was bound for the old claim on the left fork of Henderson Creek, where the boys were already. They had come over across the divide from the Indian Creek country, while he had come the roundabout way to take a look at the possibilities of getting out logs in the spring from the islands in the Yukon. He would be in to camp by six o'clock; a bit after dark, it was true, but the boys would be there, a fire would be going, and a hot supper would be ready. As for lunch, he pressed his hand against the protruding bundle under his jacket. It was also under his shirt, wrapped up in a handkerchief and lying against the naked skin. It was the only way to keep the biscuits from freezing. He smiled agreeably to himself as he thought of those biscuits, each cut open and sopped in bacon grease, and each enclosing a generous slice of fried bacon.

He plunged in among the big spruce trees. The trail was faint. A foot of snow had fallen since the last sled had passed over, and he was glad he was without a sled, travelling light. In fact, he carried nothing but the lunch wrapped in the handkerchief. He was surprised, however, at the cold. It certainly was cold, he concluded, as he rubbed his numb nose and cheekbones with his mittened hand. He was a warm-whiskered man, but the hair on his face did not protect the high cheekbones and the eager nose that thrust itself aggressively into the frosty air.

At the man's heels trotted a dog, a big native husky, the proper wolf-dog, grey-coated and without any visible or temperamental difference from its brother, the wild wolf. The animal was depressed by the tremendous cold. It knew that it was no time for travelling. Its instinct told it a truer tale than was told to the man by the man's judgement. In reality, it was not merely colder than fifty below zero; it was colder than sixty below, than seventy below. It was seventy-five below zero. Since the freezing point is thirty-two above zero, it meant that one hundred and seven degrees of frost obtained. The dog did not know anything about thermometers.

The frozen moisture of its breathing had settled on its fur in a fine powder of frost, and especially were its jowls, muzzle and eyelashes whitened by its crystal breath. The man's red beard and moustache were likewise frosted, but more solidly, the deposit taking the form of ice and increasing with every warm, moist breath he exhaled. Also, the man was chewing tobacco, and the muzzle of ice held his lips so rigidly that he was unable to clear his chin when he expelled the juice. The result was a crystal beard of the colour and solidity of amber was increasing its length on his chin. If he fell down it would shatter itself, like glass, into brittle fragments. But he did not mind the appendage. It was the penalty all tobacco chewers paid in that country, and he had been out before in two cold snaps. They had not been so cold as this, he knew, but by the spirit thermometer at Sixty Mile he knew they had been registered at fifty below and at fifty-five.

He held on through the level stretch of woods for several miles, crossed a wide flat of nigger heads, and dropped down a bank to the frozen bed of a small stream. This was Henderson Creek, and he knew he was ten miles from the forks. He looked at his watch. It was ten o'clock. He was making four miles an hour, and he calculated that he would arrive at the forks at half-past twelve. He decided to celebrate that event by eating his lunch there.

The dog dropped in again at his heels, with a tail drooping discouragement, as the man swung along the creek bed. The furrow of the old sled trail was plainly visible, but a dozen inches of snow covered up the marks of the last runners. In a month no man had come up or down that silent creek. The man held steadily on. He was not much given to thinking, and just then particularly he had nothing to think about save that he would eat lunch at the forks and that at six o'clock he would be in camp with the boys. There was nobody to talk to; and, had there been, speech would have been impossible because of the ice muzzle on his mouth. So he continued monotonously to chew tobacco and to increase the length of his amber beard.

Once in a while the thought reiterated itself that it was very cold and that he had never experienced such cold. As he walked along he rubbed his cheekbones and nose with the back of his mittened hand. He did this automatically, now and again changing hands. But, rub as he would, the instant he stopped his cheekbones went numb, and the following instant the end of his nose went numb. He was sure to frost his cheeks; he knew that, and experienced a pang of regret that he had not devised a nose strap of the sort Bud wore in cold snaps. Such a strap passed across the cheeks, as well, and saved them. But it didn't matter much, after all. What were frosted cheeks? A bit painful, that was all; they were never serious.

Empty as the man's mind was of thoughts, he was keenly observant, and he noticed the changes in the creeks, the curves and bends and timber jams, and always he sharply noted where he placed his feet. Once, coming round a bend, he shied abruptly, like a startled horse, curved away from the place where he had been walking, and retreated several paces back along the trail. The creek he knew was frozen clear to the bottom – no creek could contain water in that arctic winter – but he knew also that there were springs that bubbled out from the hillsides and ran along under the snow and on top of the ice of the creek. He knew that the coldest snaps never froze these springs, and he knew likewise their danger. They were traps. They hid pools of water under the snow that might be three inches deep, or three feet. Sometimes a skin of ice half an inch thick covered them, and in turn was covered by the snow. Sometimes there were alternate layers of water and ice skin, so that when one broke through he kept on breaking through for a while, sometimes wetting himself to the waist.

That was why he had shied in such a panic. He had felt the give under his feet and heard the crackle of a snow-hidden ice skin. And to get his feet wet in such a temperature meant trouble and danger. At the very least it meant delay, for he would be forced to stop and build a fire, and under its protection to bare his feet while he dried his socks and moccasins. He stood and studied the creek bed and its banks, and decided that the flow of water came from the right. He reflected awhile, rubbing his nose and cheeks, then skirted to the left, stepping gingerly and testing the footing for each step. Once clear of the danger, he took a fresh chew of tobacco and swung along at his four-mile gait.

In the course of the next two hours he came upon several similar traps. Usually the snow above the hidden pools had a sunken, candied appearance that advertised the danger. Once again, however, he had a close call; and once, suspecting danger, he compelled the dog to go in front. The dog did not want to go. It hung back until the man shoved it forward, and then it went quickly across the white, unbroken surface. Suddenly it broke through, floundered to one side, and got away to firmer footing. It had wet its forefeet and legs, and almost immediately the water that clung to it turned to ice. It made quick efforts to lick the ice off its legs, then dropped down in the snow and began to bite out the ice that had formed between the toes. This was a matter of instinct. To permit the ice to remain would mean sore feet. It did not know this. It merely obeyed the mysterious prompting that arose from the deep crypts of its being. But the man knew, having achieved a judgement on the subject, and he removed the mitten from his right hand and helped to tear out the ice particles. He did not expose his fingers more than a minute, and was astonished at the swift numbness that smote them. It certainly was cold. He pulled on the mitten hastily, and beat the hand savagely across his chest.

At twelve o'clock the day was at its brightest. Yet the sun was too far south on its winter journey to clear the horizon. The bulge of the earth intervened between it and Henderson Creek, where the man walked under a clear sky at noon and cast no shadow. At half-past twelve, to the minute, he arrived at the forks of the creek. He was pleased at the speed he had made. If he kept it up, he would certainly be with the boys by six. He unbuttoned his jacket and shirt and drew forth his lunch. The action consumed no more than a quarter of a minute, yet in that brief moment the numbness laid hold of the exposed fingers. He did not put the mitten on, but, instead, struck the fingers a dozen sharp smashes against his leg. Then he sat down on a snow-covered log to eat. The sting that followed upon the striking of his fingers against his leg ceased so quickly that he was startled. He had had no chance to take a bite of biscuit. He struck the fingers repeatedly and returned them to the mitten, baring the other hand for the purpose of eating. He tried to take a mouthful, but the ice muzzle prevented. He had forgotten to build a fire and thaw out. He chuckled at his foolishness, and as he chuckled he noted the numbness creeping into the exposed fingers. Also, he noted that the stinging which had first come to his toes when he sat down was already passing away. He wondered whether the toes were warm or numb. He moved them inside the moccasins and decided that they were numb.

He pulled the mitten on hurriedly and stood up. He was a bit frightened. He stamped up and down until the stinging returned into the feet. It certainly was cold, was his thought. That man from Sulphur Creek had spoken the truth when telling how cold it sometimes got in the country. And he had laughed at him at the time! That showed one must not be too sure of things. There was no mistake about it, it *was* cold. He strode up and down, stamping his feet and threshing his arms, until reassured by the returning warmth. Then he got out matches and proceeded to make a fire. From the undergrowth, where high water of the previous spring had lodged a supply of seasoned twigs, he got his firewood. Working carefully from a small beginning, he soon had a roaring fire, over which he thawed the ice from his face and in the protection of which he ate his biscuits. For the moment the cold of space was outwitted. The dog took satisfaction in the fire, stretching out close enough for warmth and far enough away to escape being singed.

When the man had finished, he filled his pipe and took his comfortable time over a smoke. Then he pulled on his mittens, settled the ear-flaps of his cap firmly about his ears, and took the creek trail up the left fork. The dog was disappointed and yearned back towards the fire. This man did not know cold. Possibly all the generations of his ancestry had been ignorant of cold, of real cold, of cold one hundred and seven degrees below freezing point. But the dog knew; all its ancestry knew, and it had inherited the knowledge. And it knew that it was not good to walk abroad in such fearful cold. It was the time to lie snug in a hole in the snow and wait for a curtain of cloud to be drawn across the face of outer space whence this cold came.

The man took a chew of tobacco and proceeded to start a new amber beard. Also, his moist breath quickly powdered with white his moustache, eyebrows and lashes. There did not seem to be so many springs on the left fork of the Henderson, and for half an hour the man saw no signs of any. And then it happened. At a place where there were no signs, where the soft, unbroken snow seemed to advertise solidity beneath, the man broke through. It was not deep. He wet himself half-way to the knees before he floundered out to the firm crust.

He was angry, and cursed his luck aloud. He had hoped to get into camp with the boys at six o'clock, and this would delay him an hour, for he would have to build a fire and dry out his footgear. This was imperative at that low temperature – he knew that much; and he turned aside to the bank, which he climbed. On top, tangled in the underbrush about the trunks of several small spruce trees, was a high-water deposit of dry firewood – sticks and twigs, principally, but also larger portions of seasoned branches and fine, dry, last year's grasses. He threw down several large pieces on top of the snow. This served for a foundation and prevented the young flame from drowning itself in the snow it otherwise would melt. The flame he got by touching a match to a small shred of birch bark that he took from his pocket. This burned even more readily than paper. Placing it on the foundation, he fed the young flame with wisps of dry grass and with the tiniest dry twigs.

He worked slowly and carefully, keenly aware of his danger. Gradually, as the flame grew stronger, he increased the size of the twigs with which he fed it. He squatted in the snow pulling the twigs out from their entanglement in the brush and feeding directly at the flame. He knew there must be no failure. When it is seventy-five below zero, a man must not fail in his first attempt to build a fire – that is, if his feet are wet. If his feet are dry, and he fails, he can run along the trail for half a mile and restore his circulation. But the circulation of wet and freezing feet cannot be restored by running when it is seventy-five below. No matter how fast he runs, the wet feet will freeze the harder.

All this the man knew. The old-timer on Sulphur Creek had told him about it the previous fall, and now he was appreciating the advice. Already all sensation had gone out of his feet. To build the fire he had been forced to remove his mittens, and the fingers had quickly gone numb. His pace of four miles an hour had kept his heart pumping blood to the surface of his body and to all the extremities. But the instant he stopped, the action of the pump eased down. The cold of space smote the unprotected tip of the planet, and he, being on that unprotected tip, received the full force of the blow. The blood of his body recoiled before it. The blood was alive, like the dog, and like the dog it wanted to hide away and cover itself up from the fearful cold. So long as he walked four miles an hour, he pumped that blood, willy-nilly, to the surface; but now it ebbed away and sank down into the recesses of his body. The extremities were the first to feel its absence. His wet feet froze the faster, and his exposed fingers numbed the faster, though they had not yet begun to freeze. Nose and cheeks were already freezing, while the skin of all his body chilled as it lost its blood.

But he was safe. Toes and nose and cheeks would be only touched by the frost, for the fire was beginning to burn with strength. He was feeding it with twigs the size of his finger. In another minute he would be able to feed it with branches the size of his wrist, and then he could remove his wet footgear, and, while it dried, he could keep his naked feet warm by the fire, rubbing them at first, of course, with snow. The fire was a success. He was safe. He remembered the advice of the old-timer on Sulphur Creek, and smiled. The old-timer had been very serious in laying down the law that no man must travel alone in the Klondike after fifty below. Well, here he was; he had had the accident; he was alone; and he had saved himself. Those old-timers were rather womanish, some of them, he thought. All a man had to do was to keep his head, and he was all right. Any man who was a man could travel alone. But it was surprising, the rapidity with which his cheeks and nose were freezing. And he had not thought his fingers could go lifeless in so short a time. Lifeless they were, for he could scarcely make them move together to grip a twig, and they seemed remote from his body and from him. When he touched a twig, he had to look and see whether or not he had hold of it. The wires were pretty well down between him and his finger ends.

All of which counted for little. There was the fire, snapping and crackling and promising life with every dancing flame. He started to untie his moccasins. They were coated with ice; the thick German socks were like sheaths of iron halfway to the knees; and the moccasin strings were like rods of steel all twisted and knotted as by some conflagration. For a moment he tugged with his numb fingers, then, realizing the folly of it, he drew his sheath knife.

But before he could cut the strings, it happened. It was his own fault or, rather, his mistake. He should not have built the fire under the spruce tree. He should have built it in the open. But it had been easier to pull the twigs from the brush and drop them directly on the fire. Now the tree under which he had done this carried a weight of snow on its boughs. No wind had blown for weeks, and each bough was fully freighted. Each time he had pulled a twig he had communicated a slight agitation to the tree – an imperceptible agitation, so far as he was concerned, but an agitation sufficient to bring about the disaster. High up in the tree one bough capsized its load of snow. This fell on the boughs beneath, capsizing them. This process continued, spreading out and involving the whole tree. It grew like an avalanche, and it descended without warning upon the man and the fire, and the fire was blotted out! Where it had burned was a mantle of fresh and disordered snow.

The man was shocked. It was as though he had just heard his own sentence of death. For a moment he sat and stared at the spot where the fire had been. Then he grew very calm. Perhaps the old-timer on Sulphur Creek was right. If he had only had a trail mate he would have been in no danger now.

The trail mate could have built the fire. Well, it was up to him to build the fire over again, and this second time there must be no failure. Even if he succeeded, he would most likely lose some toes. His feet must be badly frozen by now, and there would be some time before the second fire was ready.

Such were his thoughts, but he did not sit and think them. He was busy all the time they were passing through his mind. He made a new foundation for a fire, this time in the open, where no treacherous tree could blot it out. Next he gathered dry grasses and tiny twigs from the high-water flotsam. He could not bring his fingers together to pull them out, but he was able to gather them by the handful. In this way he got many rotten twigs and bits of green moss that were undesirable, but it was the best he could do. He worked methodically, even collecting an armful of the larger branches to be used later when the fire gathered strength. And all the while the dog sat and watched him, a certain yearning wistfulness in its eyes, for it looked upon him as the fire provider, and the fire was slow in coming.

When all was ready, the man reached in his pocket for a second piece of birch bark. He knew the bark was there, and, though he could not feel it with his fingers, he could hear its crisp rustling as he fumbled for it. Try as he would, he could not clutch hold of it. And all the time, in his consciousness, was the knowledge that each instant his feet were freezing. This thought tended to put him in a panic, but he fought against it and kept calm. He pulled on his mittens with his teeth, and threshed his arms back and forth, beating his hands with all his might against his sides. He did this sitting down, and he stood up to do it; and all the while the dog sat in the snow, its wolf brush of a tail curled around warmly over its forefront, its sharp wolf ears pricked forward intently as it watched the man. And the man, as he beat and threshed with his arms and hands, felt a great surge of envy as he regarded the creature that was warm and secure in its natural covering.

After a time he was aware of the first faraway signals of sensation in his beaten fingers. The faint tingling grew stronger till it evolved into a stinging ache that was excruciating, but which the man hailed with satisfaction. He stripped the mitten from his right hand and fetched forth the birch bark. The exposed fingers were quickly going numb again. Next he brought out his bunch of sulphur matches. But the tremendous cold had already driven the life out of his fingers. In his effort to separate one match from the others, the whole bunch fell in the snow. He tried to pick it out of the snow, but failed. The dead fingers could neither touch nor clutch. He was very careful. He drove the thought of his freezing feet, and nose, and cheeks, out of his mind, devoting his whole soul to the matches. He watched, using the sense of vision in place of that touch, and when he saw his fingers on each side the bunch, he closed them – that is, he willed to close them, for the wires were down, and the fingers did not obey. He pulled the mitten on the right hand, and beat it fiercely against his knee. Then with both mittened hands, he scooped the bunch of matches, along with much snow, into his lap. Yet he was no better off.

After some manipulation he managed to get the bunch between the heels of his mittened hands. In this fashion he carried it to his mouth. The ice crackled and snapped when by a violent effort he opened his mouth. He drew the lower jaw in, curled the upper lip out of the way, and scraped the bunch with his upper teeth in order to separate a match. He succeeded in getting one, which he dropped on his lap. He was no better off. He could not pick it up. Then he devised a way. He picked it up in his teeth and scratched it on his leg. Twenty times he scratched before he succeeded in lighting it. As it flamed he held it with his teeth to the birch bark. But the burning brimstone went up his nostrils and into his lungs, causing him to cough spasmodically. The match fell into the snow and went out.

The old-timer on Sulphur Creek was right, he thought in the moment of controlled despair that ensued: after fifty below, a man should travel with a partner. He beat his hands, but failed in exciting any sensation. Suddenly he bared both hands, removing the mittens with his teeth. He caught the whole bunch between the heels of his hands. His arm muscles not being frozen enabled him to press the hand heels tightly against the matches. Then he scratched the bunch along his leg. It flared into flame, seventy sulphur matches at once! There was no wind to blow them out. He kept his head to one side to escape the strangling fumes, and held the blazing bunch to the birch bark. As he so held it, he became aware of sensation in his hand. His flesh was burning. He could smell it. Deep down below the surface he could feel it. The sensation developed into pain that grew acute. And still he endured it, holding the flame of the matches clumsily to the bark that would not light readily because his own burning hands were in the way, absorbing most of the flame.

At last, when he could endure no more, he jerked his hands apart. The blazing matches fell sizzling into the snow, but the birch bark was alight. He began laying dry grasses and the tiniest twigs on the flame. He could not pick and choose, for he had to lift the fuel between the heels of his hands. Small pieces of rotten wood and green moss clung to the twigs, and he bit them off as well as he could with his teeth. He cherished the flame carefully and awkwardly. It meant life, and it must not perish. The withdrawal of blood from the surface of his body now made him begin to shiver, and he grew more awkward. A large piece of green moss fell squarely on the little fire. He tried to poke it out with his fingers, but his shivering frame made him poke too far, and he disrupted the nucleus of the little fire, the burning grasses and tiny twigs separating and scattering. He tried to poke them together again, but in spite of the tenseness of the effort, his shivering got away with him, and the twigs were hopelessly scattered. Each twig gushed a puff of smoke and went out. The fire provider had failed. As he looked apathetically about him, his eyes chanced on the dog, sitting across the ruins of the fire from him, in the snow, making restless, hunching movements, slightly lifting one forefoot and then the other, shifting its weight back and forth on them with wistful eagerness.

The sight of the dog put a wild idea into his head. He remembered the tale of the man, caught in a blizzard, who killed a steer and crawled inside the carcass, and so was saved. He would kill the dog and bury his hands in the warm body until the numbness went out of them. Then he could build another fire. He spoke to the dog, calling it to him; but in his voice was a strange note of fear that frightened the animal, who had never known the man to speak in such a way before. Something was the matter, and its suspicious nature sensed danger – it knew not what danger, but somewhere, somehow, in its brain arose an apprehension of the man. It flattened its ears down at the sound of the man's voice, and its restless, hunching movements and the liftings and shiftings of its fore-feet became more pronounced; but it would not come to the man. He got on his hands and knees and crawled towards the dog. This unusual posture again excited suspicion, and the animal sidled mincingly away.

The man sat up in the snow for a moment and struggled for calmness. Then he pulled on his mittens, by means of his teeth, and got upon his feet. He glanced down at first in order to assure himself that he was really standing up, for the absence of sensation in his feet left him unrelated to the earth. His erect position in itself started to drive the webs of suspicion from the dog's mind; and when he spoke peremptorily, with the sound of whip lashes in his voice, the dog rendered its customary allegiance and came to him. As it came within reaching distance, the man lost his control. His arms flashed out to the dog, and he experienced genuine surprise when he discovered that his hands could not clutch, that there was neither bend nor feeling in the fingers. He had forgotten for the moment that they were frozen and that they were freezing more and more. All this happened quickly, and before the animal could get away, he encircled its body with his arms. He sat down in the snow, and in this fashion held the dog, while it snarled and whined and struggled.

But it was all he could do, hold its body encircled in his arms and sit there. He realized he could not kill the dog. There was no way to do it. With his helpless hands he could neither draw nor hold his sheath knife nor throttle the animal. He released it, and it plunged wildly away, with tail between its legs, and still snarling. It halted forty feet away and surveyed him curiously, with ears sharply pricked forward.

The man looked down at his hands in order to locate them, and found them hanging on the ends of his arms. It struck him as curious that one should have to use his eyes in order to find out where his hands were. He began threshing his arms back and forth, beating the mittened hands against his sides. He did this for five minutes, violently, and his heart pumped enough blood up to the surface to put a stop to his shivering. But no sensation was aroused in the hands. He had an impression that they hung like weights on the ends of his arms, but when he tried to run the impression down, he could not find it.

A certain fear of death, dull and oppressive, came to him. This fear quickly became poignant as he realized that it was no longer a mere matter of freezing his fingers and toes, or of losing his hands and feet, but that it was a matter of life and death with the chances against him. This threw him into a panic, and he turned and ran up the creek bed along the old, dim trail. The dog joined in behind him and kept up with him. He ran blindly, without intention, in fear such as he had never known in his life. Slowly, as he ploughed and floundered through the snow, he began to see things again – the banks of the creek, the old timber jams, the leafless aspens, and the sky.

The running made him feel better. He did not shiver. Maybe, if he ran on, his feet would thaw out; and, anyway, if he ran far enough, he would reach camp and the boys. Without doubt he would lose some fingers and toes and some of his face; but the boys would take care of him, and save the rest of him when he got there. And at the same time there was another thought in his mind that said he would never get to the camp and the boys; that it was too many miles away, that the freezing had too great a start on him, and that he would soon be stiff and dead. This thought he kept in the background and refused to consider. Sometimes it pushed itself forward and demanded to be heard, but he thrust it back and strove to think of other things.

It struck him as curious that he could run at all on feet so frozen that he could not feel them when they struck the earth and took the weight of his body. He seemed to himself to skim along above the surface, and to have no connection with the earth. Somewhere he had once seen a winged Mercury, and he wondered if Mercury felt as he felt when skimming over the earth.

His theory of running until he reached camp and the boys had one flaw in it: he lacked the endurance. Several times he stumbled, and finally he tottered, crumpled up and fell. When he tried to rise, he failed. He must sit and rest, he decided, and next time he would merely walk and keep on going. As he sat and regained his breath, he noted that he was feeling quite warm and comfortable. He was not shivering, and it even seemed that a warm glow had come to his chest and trunk. And yet, when he touched his nose or cheeks, there was no sensation. Running would not thaw them out. Nor would it thaw out his hands and feet. Then the thought came to him that the frozen portions of his body must be extending. He tried to keep this thought down, to forget it, to think of something else; he was aware of the panicky feeling that it caused, and he was afraid of the panic. But the thought asserted itself, and persisted, until it produced a vision of his body totally frozen. This was too much, and he made another wild run along the trail. Once he slowed down to a walk, but the thought of the freezing extending itself made him run again.

And all the time the dog ran with him, at his heels. When he fell down a second time, it curled its tail over its forefeet and sat in front of him, facing him, curiously eager and intent. The warmth and security of the animal angered him, and he cursed it till it flattened down its ears appeasingly. This time the shivering came more quickly upon the man. He was losing in his battle with the frost. It was creeping into his body from all sides. The thought of it drove him on, but he ran no more than a hundred feet, when he staggered and pitched headlong. It was his last panic. When he had recovered his breath and control, he sat up and entertained in his mind the conception of meeting death with dignity. However, the conception did not come to him in such terms. His idea of it was that he had been making a fool of himself, running around like a chicken with its head off – such was the simile that occurred to him. Well, he was bound to freeze anyway, and he might as well take it decently. With this new-found peace of mind came the first glimmerings of drowsiness. A good idea, he thought, to sleep off to death. It was like taking an anaesthetic. Freezing was not so bad as people thought. There were lots worse worse ways to die.

He pictured the boys finding his body next day. Suddenly he found himself with them, coming along the trail looking for himself. And, still with them, he came around a turn in the trail and found himself lying in the snow. He did not belong with himself any more, for even then he was out of himself, standing with the boys and looking at himself in the snow. It certainly was cold, was his thought. When he got back to the States he could tell the folks what real cold was. He drifted on from this to a vision of the old-timer on Sulphur Creek. He could see him quite clearly, warm and comfortable, and smoking a pipe.

'You were right, old hoss; you were right,' the man mumbled to the old-timer of Sulphur Creek.

Then the man drowsed off into what seemed to him the most comfortable and satisfying sleep he had ever known. The dog sat facing him and waiting. The brief day drew to a close in a long, slow twilight. There were no signs of a fire to be made, and, besides, never in the dog's experience had it known a man to sit like that in the snow and make no fire. As the twilight drew on, its eager yearning for the fire mastered it, and with a great lifting and shifting of forefeet, it whined softly, then flattened its ears down in anticipation of being chidden by the man. But the man remained silent. Later the dog whined loudly. And still later it crept close to the man and caught the scent of death. This made the animal bristle and back away. A little longer it delayed, howling under the stars that leaped and danced and shone brightly in the cold sky. Then it turned and trotted up the trail in the direction of the camp it knew, where

Jack London were the other food providers and fire providers.

Cave-building   People in our part of the country prefer living in caves. This is largely because our loess soil makes cave-building easy and the result is a nicer and better insulated dwelling than an ordinary house. I must have built a good forty caves in my day. My father taught me how to build them, but I'm no specialist. Anybody can build a cave.

There are two kinds of cave: earth ones and stone ones. The earth caves are dug into the hillside. The first thing to do is to find a place with the right kind of soil, hard yellow loess soil. You cannot build a cave where the soil is sandy. There are lots of places in this valley suitable for building caves. But you can make a mistake. Li Hsiu-tang made one this year when he began building a big cave down at the bottom of the eastern side of Naopanshan behind Chang Chung-wen's pigsty. The earth was damp there and all he achieved was a big hole. The higher up the hillside you dig your cave the better the earth usually is; but it means you have a longer way to the well.

You don't need so many people to build an earthen cave. An ordinary cave of normal size, 18 to 19 chi long, 9 to 10 chi high and 8 to 9 chi wide, including making the kang and cooking stove and chimney, takes about forty work-days. A house of the same size takes the same or a little less, but it isn't so practical and costs more to heat.

Having selected a place where the earth seems to be of the right kind, you smooth the hillside so that you have a vertical face. In doing this you will see what the soil is like to work with. Next, you make a first hole of two by seven chi and dig in for roughly three chi before you start enlarging. As you dig, the kind of soil will show you how large you can make the cave. The harder and closer the soil is, the larger you can make your cave, and vice versa. Having dug out your cave, you polish the earth walls to make them smooth, then you plaster them with mud made of loess earth. All this time, you leave the outer wall untouched, using just the little opening that you made at the beginning, but once the cave is finished you open up this wall so that you have a door and a window. The window is a lattice frame with paper stretched over it. This makes a good window that lets in the light, but keeps out the wind. Nowadays we also use glass a bit; but glass is expensive and it is seldom one sees a piece more than two by three chi. Besides, glass is not always practical, and it calls for a considerably more complicated structure for the lattice.

At first, caves are slightly damp, but they dry out after three or five months. If the soil is of good quality and hard and firm, you can then build additional caves and store-rooms leading off from the first cave. But if you do that, you make the passages between them rather narrow, roughly two by seven chi.

You cannot build this sort of cave by yourself. It needs several of you. We usually exchange work and help each other. Up here in northern Shensi people prefer, as I said, to live in caves, because they are warmer in winter and cooler in summer; but down in central Shensi people prefer to live in houses.

But earth caves don't last well, and they can also be dangerous. Even if the soil is of good quality, an earth cave seldom lasts more than two or three generations. Often only thirty years. If the soil is poor and you have help enough to be able to build a whole-stone cave, you can build one that is half and half: half-stone cave and half-earth cave dug into the hillside. But that is not a good solution. You can tell when an earth cave is nearing the end of its days, because then small pieces begin falling from the roof. You have to be careful when that happens; but you can still use the cave, if you strengthen it.

There are two ways of strengthening. The best method, though one that can only be used for smaller caves, is to take six-inch planks that you soften and bend in steam and fix these up under the curve of the roof one chi apart. These make a good support and the cave can be used for a long time yet. The other method – you saw it used in Yen Chi-yung's cave, he's a carpenter and knows how to do it – is to build a framework with support pillars and stretchers and cross-beams to hold up the roof. But this isn't very practical and it doesn't last either.

Stone caves are better. I have built a number of them. Twenty years ago I planned all the stone caves of Liu Ling's basic school and was in charge of building them. I also was in charge when the three caves we are sitting in now were built. A stone cave calls for more careful planning and considerably more work. You can take it that each stone cave takes roughly four hundred work-days. The three caves in this row took the work of seventy men for a whole month. They are thus considerably more expensive to build than both earth caves and ordinary houses; but, while an ordinary house won't go more than thirty years without major repairs, a stone cave will stand for four or five hundred years and not need a thing doing to it. In theory stone caves are indestructible. The only thing requiring maintenance is the paper and woodwork of the windows, for wood will rot in time. But in an ordinary house there is a lot that can rot and fall and need replacing.

In principle, it is best for a cave to face south, because then it will be warmed by the winter sun, which hangs low, and the summer sun, which stands high in the sky, won't reach in; but you cannot pay much attention to that, where earth or stone caves are concerned, for they have to be sited according to the condition of the ground. I have built caves facing all quarters of the compass, but, wherever I could, I have avoided making them face east or west.

Caves, of course, are built with cooking stoves and chimneys, but with both earth and stone caves we usually make an additional outside kitchen for use in summer. That helps to keep the cave cool in summer and the women consider it an advantage to be able to work outdoors. When we do this, we site the outside kitchen in a shady place.

In many places you have to be careful about drainage when building stone caves, but here with us the subsoil water is fairly far down and we have good stone. We have not needed any special drainage either at the school or for this row. We begin by digging the foundations. We excavate ten chi down. The hole corresponds to the outside measurements of the cave-to-be. Then we make a foundation of tamped loess. If this is done carefully, it becomes almost as hard as concrete. On this foundation we build two stone walls, which are the inner long walls of the cave. We make a stone floor. When these inner walls reach a height of six chi above the stone floors we build the inner short walls. Then we reckon out the vault. This has to be a semi-circle and rest on the two inner long walls. We don't calculate with paper and brush. We are farmers and we cannot write or calculate on paper; but we know how it has to be. The inner short wall is a measure for the vault. We put up a frame in the cave and build the vault with stones. This calls for a lot of work, for each stone has to be cut so that it fits exactly. But you soon learn to tell from looking at a stone how it has to be done.

Once the vaulting is finished the cave will stand for hundreds of years. After that we build the outside walls. The smallest distance between the inside of the outer wall and the outside of the inner wall is five chi. The same goes for the distance between the outsides of the inner walls, if one is building several caves one beside the other as in this row. This intervening space is filled with tamped loess. The outside walls of the cave are built up six chi, plus the height of the vault, plus five chi, because the vault has also to be covered with trodden loess. Here too, five chi is the smallest permissible distance between the highest point of the vault and the top of the layer of beaten loess.

Built in this way, the roof needs no maintenance; and, although grass grows on it and we let our goats graze there, no damp can get into the cave. For the sake of drainage we make the roof slope inwards and make a gutter of baked clay there to take the water away. Neither rain nor frost nor weeds can crack the roof. Up in the north, however, where they build similar caves, but of sun-dried bricks, which aren't strong enough to bear the load, the clay roof has to be trodden every year.

We have good stone here. We took some from the old temple when it collapsed; and the rest we quarried over there where the latrines now are. You can see from the look of the hillside that we have used it as a quarry. You build several stone caves at a time, if you can; because it is cheaper to build them in a line, since that saves outer walls.

The last thing to be done to a stone cave is to plaster the walls with fine wet loess mixed with chopped straw and then whitewash them. After that, with the trellis for the window in place and the paper over it, and the door made, it is a good dwelling and one that is easy to keep warm in winter, while it is always cool in summer. And you never need to think about maintenance.

We are planning to rebuild the whole village with stone caves down here; but that is a long-term plan. We haven't yet decided exactly where we are going to build. That also depends on whether we are to get a better water-supply. The well here is not as good as it might be. But we have decided in principle to start building the first range in 1963 and 1964. In a few years the whole village will consist of stone caves and they will stand for five hundred years without needing repair. That is what makes stone caves the most economical.

Translated from the Chinese by Jan Myrdal
Mau Ke-yeh

Lost in the Desert I began a slow descent, intending to slip under the mass of clouds. Meanwhile I had had a look at my map. One thing was sure – the land below me lay at sea-level, and there was no risk of conking against a hill. Down I went, flying due north so that the lights of the cities would strike square into my windows. I must have overflown them, and should therefore see them on my left.

Now I was flying below the cumulus. But alongside was another cloud hanging lower down on the left. I swerved so as not to be caught in its net, and headed north-north-east. This second cloud-bank certainly went down a long way, for it blocked my view of the horizon. I dared not give up any more altitude. My altimeter registered twelve thousand feet, but I had no notion of the atmospheric pressure here. Prévot leaned toward me and I shouted to him: 'I'm going out to sea. I'd rather come down on it than risk a crash here.'

As a matter of fact, there was nothing to prove that we had not drifted over the sea already. Below that cloud-bank visibility was exactly nil. I hugged my window, trying to read below me, to discover flares, signs of life. I was a man raking dead ashes, trying in vain to retrieve the flame of life in a hearth.

'A lighthouse!'

Both of us spied it at the same moment, that winking decoy! What madness! Where was that phantom light, that invention of the night? For at the very second when Prévot and I leaned forward to pick it out of the air where it had glittered nine-hundred feet below our wings, suddenly, at that very instant. . . .

'Oh!'

I am quite sure that this was all I said. I am quite sure that all I felt was a terrific crash that rocked our world to its foundations. We had crashed against the earth at a hundred and seventy miles an hour. I am quite sure that in the split second that followed, all I expected was the great flash of ruddy light of the explosion in which Prévot and I were to be blown up together. Neither he nor I had felt the least emotion of any kind. All I could observe in myself was an extraordinary tense feeling of expectancy, the expectancy of that resplendent star in which we were to vanish within the second.

But there was no ruddy star. Instead there was a sort of earthquake that splintered our cabin, ripped away the windows, blew sheets of metal hurtling through space a hundred yards away, and filled our very entrails with its roar. The ship quivered like a knife blade thrown from a distance into a block of oak, and its anger mashed us as if we were so much pulp.

One second, two seconds passed, and the plane still quivered while I waited with grotesque impatience for the forces within it to burst like a bomb. But the subterranean quakings went on without a climax of eruption while I marvelled uncomprehendingly at its invisible travail. I was baffled by the quaking, the anger, the interminable postponement. Five seconds passed; six seconds. And suddenly we were seized by a spinning motion, a shock that jerked our cigarettes out of the window, pulverized the starboard wing – and then nothing, nothing but a frozen immobility. I shouted to Prévot:

'Jump!'

And in that instant he cried out:

'Fire!'

We dived together through the wrecked window and found ourselves standing side by side, sixty feet from the plane.
I said:

'Are you hurt?'

He answered:

'Not a bit.'

But he was rubbing his knee.

'Better run your hands over yourself,' I said; 'move about a bit. Sure no bones are broken?'

He answered:

'I'm all right. It's that emergency pump.'

Emergency pump! I was sure he was going to keel over any minute and split open from head to navel there before my eyes. But he kept repeating with a glassy stare:

'That pump, that emergency pump.'

He's out of his head, I thought. He'll start dancing in a minute.

Finally he stopped staring at the plane – which had not gone up in flames – and stared at me instead. And he said again:

'I'm all right. It's that emergency pump. It got me in the knee.'

Why we were not blown up I do not know. I switched on my electric torch and went back over the furrow in the ground traced by the plane. Two hundred and fifty yards from where we stopped the ship had begun to shed the twisted iron and sheet-metal that spattered the sand the length of her traces. We were to see, when day came, that we had run almost tangentially into a gentle slope at the top of a barren plateau. At the point of impact there was a hole in the sand that looked as if it had been made by a plough. Maintaining an even keel, the plane had run its course with the fury and the tail-lashings of a reptile gliding on its belly at the rate of a hundred and seventy miles an hour. We owed our lives to the fact that this desert was surfaced with round black pebbles which had rolled over and over like ball-bearings beneath us. They must have rained upward to the heavens as we shot through them.

Prévot disconnected the batteries for fear of fire by short-circuit. I leaned against the motor and turned the situation over my mind. I had been flying high for four hours and a quarter, possibly with a thirty-mile following wind. I had been jolted a good deal. If the wind had changed since the weather people forecast it, I was unable to say into what quarter it had veered. All I could make out was that we had crashed in an empty square two hundred and fifty miles on each side.

Prévot came up and sat down beside me.

'I can't believe that we're alive,' he said. . . .

We crawled into the cabin and waited for dawn. I stretched out, and as I settled down to sleep I took stock of our situation. We didn't know where we were; we had less than a quart of liquid between us; if we were not too far off the Benghazi–Cairo lane we should be found in a week, and that would be too late. Yet it was the best we could hope for. If, on the other hand, we had drifted off our course, we shouldn't be found in six months. One thing was sure – we could not count on being picked up by a plane; the men who came out for us would have two thousand miles to cover.

'You know, it's a shame,' Prévot said suddenly.

'What's a shame?'

'That we didn't crash properly and have it over with.' . . .

Prévot and I walked along the slopes of rolling mounds. The ground was sand covered over with a single layer of shining black pebbles. They gleamed like metal scales and all the domes about us shone like coats of mail. We had dropped down into a mineral world and were hemmed in by iron hills. . . .

We walked on for five hours and then the landscape changed. A river of sand seemed to be running through a valley, and we followed this river-bed, taking long strides in order to cover as much ground as possible and get back to the plane before night fell, if our march was in vain. Suddenly I stopped.

'Prévot!'

'What's up?'

'Our tracks!'

How long was it since we had forgotten to leave a wake behind us? We had to find it or die.

We went back, bearing to the right. When we had gone back far enough we would make a right angle to the left and eventually intersect our tracks where we had still remembered to mark them.

This we did and were off again. The heat rose and with it came the mirages. But these were still the commonplace kind – sheets of water that materialized and then vanished as we neared them. We decided to cross the valley of sand and climb the highest dome in order to look round the horizon. This was after six hours of march in which, striding along, we must have covered twenty miles.

When we had struggled up to the top of the black hump we sat down and looked at each other. At our feet lay our valley of sand opening into a desert of sand whose dazzling brightness seared our eyes. As far as the eye could see lay empty space. But in that space the play of light created mirages which, this time, were of a disturbing kind, fortresses and minarets, angular geometric hulks. I could see also a black mass that pretended to be vegetation, overhung by the last of those clouds that dissolve during the day only to return at night. This mass of vegetation was the shadow of a cumulus.

It was no good going on. The experiment was a failure. We should have to go back to our plane, to that red-and-white beacon which, perhaps, would be picked out by a flyer. I was not staking great hopes on a rescue party, but it did seem to me our last chance of salvation. In any case, we had to get back to our few drops of liquid, for our throats were parched. We were imprisoned in this iron circle, captives of the curt dictatorship of thirst.

And yet, how hard it was to turn back when there was a chance that we might be on the road to life! Beyond the mirages the horizon was perhaps rich in veritable treasures, in meadows and runnels of sweet water. I knew I was doing the right thing by returning to the plane, and yet as I swung round and started back I was filled with portents of disaster.

We were resting on the ground beside the plane. Nearly forty miles of wandering this day. The last drop of liquid had been drained. No sign of life had appeared to the east. No plane had soared overhead. How long should we be able to hold out? Already our thirst was terrible. . . .

There was still no sign that we were being sought; or rather they were doubtless hunting for us elsewhere, probably in Arabia. We were to hear no sound of plane until the day after we abandoned our own. And if ships did pass overhead, what could that mean to us? What could they see in us except two black dots among the thousand shadowy dots in the desert? Absurd to think of being distinguishable from them. When searchers have to cover two thousand miles of territory, it takes them a good two weeks to spot a plane in the desert from the sky.

They were probably looking for us all along the line from Tripoli to Persia. And still with all this, I clung to the slim chance that they might pick us out. Was that not our only chance of being saved? I changed my tactics, determining to go reconnoitring by myself.

So off I went without knowing whether or not I should have the stamina to come back. I remembered what I knew about this Libyan desert. When, in the Sahara, humidity is still at 40 per cent of saturation, it is only 18 here in Libya. Life here evaporates like a vapour. Bedouins, explorers and colonial officers all tell us that a man may go nineteen hours without water. Thereafter his eyes fill with light, and that marks the beginning of the end. The progress made by thirst is swift and terrible. But this north-east wind, this abnormal wind that had blown us out off our course and had marooned us on this plateau, was now prolonging our lives. What was the length of the reprieve it would grant us before our eyes began to fill with light? I went forward with the feeling of a man canoeing in mid-ocean.

I will admit that at daybreak this landscape seemed to me less infernal, and that I began my walk with my hands in my pockets, like a tramp on a high road. The evening before we had set snares at the mouths of certain mysterious burrows in the ground, and the poacher in me was on the alert. I went first to have a look at our traps. They were empty.

Well, this meant that I should not be drinking blood today; and indeed I hadn't expected to. But though I was not disappointed, my curiosity was aroused. What was there in the desert for these animals to live on? These were certainly the holes of fennecs, a long-eared carnivorous sand-fox the size of a rabbit. I spotted the tracks made by one of them, and gave way to the impulse to follow them. They led to a narrow stream of sand where each footprint was plainly outlined and where I marvelled at the pretty palm formed by the three toes spread fanwise in the sand.

I could imagine my little friend trotting blithely along at dawn and licking the dew off the rocks. Here the tracks were wider apart: my fennec had broken into a run. And now I see that a companion had joined him and they have trotted on side by side. These signs of a morning stroll gave me a strange thrill. They were signs of life, and I loved them for that: I almost forgot that I was thirsty. . . .

I went on, finally, and the time came when, along with my weariness, something in me began to change. If those were not mirages, I was inventing them.

'Hi! Hi, there!'

I shouted and waved my arms, but the man I had seen waving at me turned out to be a black rock. Everything in the desert had grown animate. I stopped to waken a sleeping Bedouin and he turned into the trunk of a black tree. A tree-trunk? Here in the desert? I was amazed and bent over to lift a broken bough. It was solid marble.

Straightening up I looked round and saw more black marble. An antediluvian forest littered the ground with its broken tree-tops. How many thousand years ago, under what hurricane of the time of Genesis, had this cathedral of wood crumbled in this spot? Countless centuries had rolled these fragments of giant pillars at my feet, polished them like steel, petrified and vitrified them and imbued them with the colour of jet.

I could distinguish the knots in their branches, the twistings of their once living boughs, could count the rings of life in them. This forest had rustled with birds and been filled with music that now was struck by doom and frozen into salt. And all this was hostile to me. Blacker than the chainmail of the hummocks, these solemn derelicts rejected me. What had I, a living man, to do with this incorruptible stone? Perishable as I was, I whose body was to crumble into dust, what place had I in this eternity?

Since yesterday I had walked nearly fifty miles. This dizziness
that I felt came doubtless from my thirst. Or from the sun. It
glittered on these hulks until they shone as if smeared with oil.

tortoise shell It blazed down on this universal carapace. Sand and fox had no
life here, but only a gigantic anvil on which the sun beat down.
I strode across this anvil and at my temples I could feel the
hammer-strokes of the sun.

'Hi! Hi, there!' I called out.

'There is nothing there,' I told myself. 'Take it easy. You are
delirious.'

I had to talk to myself aloud, had to bring myself to reason. It
was hard for me to reject what I was seeing, hard not to run
towards that caravan plodding on the horizon. There! Do you
see it?

'Fool! You know very well that you are inventing it.'

'You mean that nothing in the world is real?' . . .

Over the hilltop. Look there, at the horizon! The most
beautiful city in the world!

'You know perfectly well that is a mirage.'

Of course I know it is a mirage! Am I the sort of man who can
be fooled? But what if I *want* to go after that mirage? Suppose
I enjoy indulging my hope? Suppose it suits me to love that
crenellated town all beflagged with sunlight? What if I choose
to walk straight ahead on light feet? – for you must know that I
have dropped my weariness behind me, I am happy now . . .
Prévot and his gun! Don't make me laugh! I prefer my
drunkenness. I am drunk. I am dying of thirst.

It took the twilight to sober me. Suddenly I stopped, appalled
to think how far I was from our base. In the twilight the
mirage was dying. The horizon had stripped itself of its pomp,
its palaces, its priestly vestments. It was the old desert horizon
again.

'A fine day's work you've done! Night will overtake you. You
won't be able to go on before daybreak, and by that time your
tracks will have been blown away and you'll be properly
nowhere.'

In that case I may as well walk straight on. Why turn back?
Why should I bring my ship round when I may find the sea

straight ahead of me?

'When did you catch a glimpse of that sea? What makes you think you could walk that far? Meanwhile there's Prévot watching for you beside the *Simoon*. He may have been picked up by a caravan, for all you know.'

Very good. I'll go back. But first I want to call out for help.

'Hi! Hi!'

By God! You can't tell me this planet is not inhabited. Where are its men?

'Hi! Hi!'

I was hoarse. My voice was gone. I knew it was ridiculous to croak like this, but – one more try:

'Hi! Hi!'

And I turned back.

I had been walking two hours when I saw the flames of the bonfire that Prévot, frightened by my long absence, had sent up. They mattered very little to me now.

Another hour of trudging. Five hundred yards away. A hundred yards. Fifty yards.

'Good Lord!'

Amazement stopped me in my tracks. Joy surged up and filled my heart with its violence. In the firelight stood Prévot, talking to two Arabs who were leaning against the motor. He had not noticed me, for he was too full of his own joy. If only I had sat still and waited with him! I should have been saved already. Exultantly I called out:

'Hi! Hi!'

The two Bedouins gave a start and stared at me. Prévot left them standing and came forward to meet me. I opened my arms to him. He caught me by the elbow. Did he think I was keeling over? I said:

'At last, eh?'

'What do you mean?'

'The Arabs!'

'What Arabs?'

'Those Arabs there, with you.'

Prévot looked at me queerly, and when he spoke I felt as if he was reluctantly confiding a great secret to me:

'There are no Arabs here.'

This time I know I am going to cry.

A man can go nineteen hours without water, and what have we drunk since last night? A few drops of dew at dawn. But the north-east wind is still blowing, still blowing up the process of our evaporation. To it, also, we owe the continued accumulation of high clouds. If only they would drift straight overhead and break into rain! But it never rains in the desert.

'Look here, Prévot. Let's rip up one of the parachutes and spread the sections out on the ground, weighed down with stones. If the wind stays in the same quarter till morning, they'll catch the dew and we can wring them out into one of the tanks.'

We spread six triangular sections of parachute under the stars, and Prévot unhooked a fuel tank. This was as much as we could do for ourselves till dawn. But, miracle of miracles! Prévot had come upon an orange while working over the tank. We share it, and though it was little enough to men who could have used a few gallons of sweet water, still I was overcome with relief.

Stretched out beside the fire I looked at the glowing fruit and said to myself that men did not know what an orange was. 'Here we are, condemned to death,' I said to myself, 'and still the certainty of dying cannot compare with the pleasure I am feeling. The joy I take from this half of an orange which I am holding in my hand is one of the greatest joys I have ever known.'

I lay flat on my back, sucking my orange and counting the shooting stars. Here I was, for one minute infinitely happy. 'Nobody can know anything of the world in which the individual moves and has his being,' I reflected. 'There is no guessing it. Only the man locked up in it can know what it is.'

For the first time I understood the cigarette and glass of rum that are handed to the criminal about to be executed. I used to think that for a man to accept these wretched gifts at the foot of the gallows was beneath human dignity. Now I was learning that he took pleasure from them. People thought him courageous when he smiled as he smoked or drank. I knew now that he smiled because the taste gave him pleasure. People could not see that his perspective had changed, and that for him the last hour of his life was a life in itself.

We collected an enormous quantity of water – perhaps as much as two quarts. Never again would we be thirsty! We were saved: we had a liquid to drink!

I dipped my tin cup into the tank and brought up a beautiful yellow-green liquid the first mouthful of which nauseated me so that despite my thirst I had to catch my breath before swallowing it. I would have swallowed mud, I swear; but this taste of poisonous metal cut keener than thirst.

I glanced at Prévot and saw him going round and round with his eyes fixed to the ground as if looking for something. Suddenly he leaned forward and began to vomit without interrupting his spinning. Half a minute later it was my turn. I was seized by such convulsions that I went down on my knees and dug my fingers into the sand while I puked. Neither of us spoke, and for a quarter of an hour we remained thus shaken, bringing up nothing but a little bile.

After a time it passed and all I felt was a vague, distant nausea. But our last hope had fled. Whether our bad luck was due to a sizing on the parachute or to the magnesium lining of the tank, I never found out. Certain it was that we needed either another set of cloths or another receptacle.

Well, it was broad daylight and time we were on our way. This time we should strike out as fast as we could, leave this cursed plateau, and tramp till we dropped in our tracks. . . .

Night fell. The moon had swollen since I last saw it. Prévot was still not back. I stretched out on my back and turned these few data over in my mind. A familiar impression came over me and I tried to seize it. I was . . . I was . . . I was at sea. I was on a ship going to South America and was stretched out, exactly like this, on the boat deck. The tip of the mast was swaying to and fro, very slowly, among the stars. That mast was missing tonight, but again I was at sea, bound for a port I was to make without raising a finger. Slave-traders had flung me on this ship.

I thought of Prévot who was still not back. Not once had I heard him complain. That was a good thing. To hear him whine would have been unbearable. Prévot was a man.

What was that? Five hundred yards ahead of me I could see the light of his lamp. He had lost his way. I had no lamp with which to signal back. I stood up and shouted, but he could not hear me.

A second lamp, and then a third! God in Heaven! It was a search party and it was for me they were hunting!

'Hi! Hi!' I shouted.

But they had not heard me. The three lamps were still signalling me.

'Tonight I am sane,' I said to myself. 'I am relaxed. I am not out of my head. Those are certainly three lamps and they are about five hundred yards off.' I stared at them and shouted again, and again I gathered that they could not hear me.

Then for the first and only time, I was really seized with panic. I could still run, I thought. 'Wait! Wait!' I screamed. They seemed to be turning away from me, going off, hunting me elsewhere! And I stood tottering, tottering on the brink of life when there were arms out there ready to catch me! I shouted and screamed again and again.

They had heard me! An answering shout had come. I was strangling, suffocating, but I ran on, shouting as I ran, until I saw Prévot and keeled over.

When I could speak again I said: 'Whew! When I saw all those lights. . . .'

'What lights?'

God in Heaven, it was true! He was alone!

This time I was beyond despair. I was filled with a sort of dumb fury.

'What about your lake?' I rasped.

'As fast as I moved towards it, it moved back. I walked after it for about half an hour. Then it seemed still too far away, so I came back. But I am positive, now, that it is a lake.'

'You're crazy. Absolutely crazy. Why did you do it? Tell me. Why?'

What had he done, Why had he done it? I was ready to weep with indignation, yet I scarcely knew why I was so indignant. Prévot mumbled his excuse:

'I felt I had to find some water. You . . . your lips were awfully pale.'

Well! My anger died within me. I passed my hand over my forehead as if I were walking out of sleep. I was suddenly sad. I said:

'There was no mistake about it. I saw them as clearly as I see you now. Three lights there were. I tell you, Prévot, I saw them!'

Prévot made no comment.

'Well,' he said finally, 'I guess we're in a bad way.'

In this air devoid of moisture the soil is swift to give off its temperature. It was already very cold. I stood up and stamped about. But soon a violent fit of trembling came over me. My dehydrated blood was moving sluggishly and I was pierced by a freezing chill which was not merely the chill of night. My teeth were chattering and my whole body had begun to twitch. My hand shook so that I could not hold an electric torch. I who had never been sensitive to cold was about to die of cold. What a strange effect thirst can have!

Somewhere, tired of carrying it in the sun, I had let my waterproof drop. Now the wind was growing bitter and I was learning that in the desert there is no place of refuge. The desert is as smooth as marble. By day it throws no shadow; by night it hands you over naked to the wind. Not a tree, not a hedge, not a rock behind which I could seek shelter. The wind was charging me like a troop of cavalry across open country. I turned and twisted to escape it: I lay down, stood up, lay down again, and still I was exposed to its freezing lash. I had no strength to run from the assassin and under the sabre stroke I tumbled to my knees, my head between my hands.

A little later I pieced these bits together and remembered that I had struggled to my feet and had started to walk on, shivering as I went. I had started forward wondering where I was and then I had heard Prévot. His shouting had jolted me into consciousness.

I went back toward him, still trembling from head to foot – quivering with attack of hiccups that was convulsing my whole body. To myself I said: 'It isn't the cold. It's something else. It's the end.' The simple fact was that I hadn't enough water in me. I had tramped too far yesterday and the day before when I was off by myself, and I was dehydrated.

The thought of dying of the cold hurt me. I preferred the phantoms of my mind, the trees, the lamps. At least they would have killed me by enchantment. But to be whipped to death like a slave! . . .

Confound it! Down on my knees again! We had with us a little store of medicines – a hundred grammes of 90 per cent alcohol, the same of pure ether and a small bottle of iodine. I tried to swallow a little of the ether: it was like swallowing a knife. Then I tried the alcohol: it contracted my gullet. I dug a pit in the sand, lay down in it, and flung handfuls of sand over me until all but my face was buried in it.

Prévot was able to collect a few twigs, and he lit a fire which soon burnt itself out. He wouldn't bury himself in the sand, but preferred to stamp round and round in a circle. That was foolish.

My throat stayed shut, and though I knew that was a bad sign, I felt better. I felt calm. I felt a peace that was beyond all hope. Once more, despite myself, I was journeying, trussed up on the deck of my slave ship under the stars. It seemed to me that I was perhaps not in such a bad pass after all.

So long as I lay absolutely motionless, I no longer felt the cold. This allowed me to forget my body buried in the sand. I said to myself that I would not budge an inch, and would therefore never suffer again.

A little while ago the wind had been after me with whip and spur, and I was running in circles like a frightened fox. After that came a time when I couldn't breathe. A great knee was crushing in my chest. A knee. I was writhing in vain to free myself from the weight of an angel who had overthrown me. There had not been a moment when I was alone in this desert. But now I have ceased to believe in my surroundings. . . .

The sky seemed to me faintly bright. I drew up one arm through the sand. There was a bit of torn parachute within reach, and I ran my hand over it. It was bone-dry. Let's see. Dew falls at dawn. Here was dawn risen and no moisture on the cloth. My mind was befuddled and I heard myself say: 'There is a dry heart here, a dry heart that cannot know the relief of tears.'

I scrambled to my feet. 'We're off, Prévot,' I said. 'Our throats are still open. Get along, man!'

The wind that shrivels up a man in nineteen hours was now blowing out of the west. My gullet was not yet shut, but it was hard and painful and I could feel that there was a rasp in it. Soon that cough would begin that I had been told about and was now expecting. My tongue was becoming a nuisance. But most serious of all, I was beginning to see shining spots before my eyes. When those spots changed into flames, I should simply lie down.

The first morning hours were cool and we took advantage of them to get on at a good pace. We knew that once the sun was high there would be no more walking for us. We no longer had the right to sweat. Certainly not to stop and catch our breath. This coolness was merely the coolness of low humidity. The prevailing wind was coming from the desert, and under its soft and treacherous caress the blood was being dried out of us.

Our first day's nourishment had been a few grapes. In the next three days each of us ate half an orange and a bit of cake. If we had had anything left now, we couldn't have eaten it, because we had no saliva with which to masticate it. But I had stopped being hungry. Thirsty I was, yes, and it seemed to me that I was suffering less from thirst itself than from the effects of thirst. Gullet hard. Tongue like plaster of Paris. A rasping in the throat. A horrible taste in the mouth. . . .

We had sat down after all, but it could not be for long. Nevertheless, it was impossible to go five hundred yards without our legs giving way. To stretch out on the sand would be marvellous – but it could not be. . . .

I swear to you that something is about to happen. I swear that life has sprung in this desert. I swear that this emptiness, this stillness, has suddenly become more stirring than a tumult on a public square.

'Prévot! Footprints! We are saved!'

We had wandered from the trail of the human species; we had cast ourselves forth from the tribe; we had found ourselves alone on earth and forgotten by the universal migration; and here, imprinted in the sand, were the divine and naked feet of man!

'Look, Prévot, here two men stood together and then separated.'

'Here a camel knelt.'

'Here. . . .'

But it was not true that we were already saved. It was not
enough to squat down and wait. Before long we should be past
saving. Once the cough had begun, the progress made by thirst
is swift.

Still, I believed in that caravan swaying somewhere in the
desert, heavy with its cargo of treasure.

We went on. Suddenly I heard a cock crow. . . .

'Did you hear that?'

'What?'

'The cock.'

'Why . . . why, yes, I did.'

To myself I said: 'Fool! Get it through your head! This means
life!'

I had one last hallucination – three dogs chasing one another.
Prévot looked, but could not see them. However, both of us
waved our arms at a Bedouin. Both of us shouted with all the
breath in our bodies, and laughed for happiness.

But our voices could not carry thirty yards. The Bedouin on his
slow-moving camel had come into view from behind a dune
and now he was moving slowly out of sight. The man was
probably the only Arab in this desert, sent by a demon to
materialize and vanish before the eyes of us who could not run.

We saw in profile on the dune another Arab. We shouted, but
our shouts were whispers. We waved our arms and it seemed to
us that they must fill the sky with monstrous signals. Still the
Bedouin stared with averted face away from us.

At last, slowly, slowly he began a right-angle turn in our
direction. At the very second when he came face to face with
us, I thought, the curtain would come down. At the very
second when his eyes met ours, thirst would vanish and by this
man would death and the mirages be wiped out. Let this man
but make a quarter turn left and the world is changed. Let him
bring his torso round, but sweep the scene with a glance, and
like a god he can create life.

The miracle had come to pass. He was walking towards us over
the sand like a god over the waves.

Wind, Sand and Stars
Translated from the
French by
Lewis Galentière
**Antoine de
Saint-Exupéry**

A Slave Becomes a Runaway

There are some things about life I don't understand. Everything about Nature is obscure to me, and about the gods more so still. The gods are capricious and wilful, and they are the cause of many strange things which happen here and which I have seen for myself. I can remember as a slave I spent half my time gazing up at the sky because it looked so painted. Once it suddenly turned the colour of a hot coal, and there was a terrible drought. Another time there was an eclipse of the sun which started at four in the afternoon and could be seen all over the island. The moon looked as if it was fighting with the sun. I noticed that everything seemed to be going backwards – it got darker and darker, and then lighter and lighter. Hens flew up to roost. People were too frightened to speak. Some died of heart failure and others were struck dumb.

I saw the same thing happen again in different places, but I never dreamed of trying to find out why. You see, I know it all depends on Nature, everything comes from Nature, even what can't be seen. We men cannot do such things because we are the subjects of a God; of Jesus Christ, who is the one most talked about. Jesus Christ wasn't born in Africa, he came from Nature herself, as the Virgin Mary was a señorita.

The strongest gods are African. I tell you it's certain they could fly and they did what they liked with their witchcraft. I don't know how they permitted slavery. The truth is, I start thinking, and I can't make head or tail of it. To my mind it all started with the scarlet handkerchiefs, the day they crossed the wall. There was an old wall in Africa, right round the coast, made of palm-bark and magic insects which stung like the devil. For years they frightened away all the whites who tried to set foot in Africa. It was the scarlet which did for the Africans; both the kings and the rest surrendered without a struggle. When the kings saw that the whites – I think the Portuguese were the first – were taking out these scarlet handkerchiefs as if they were waving, they told the blacks, 'Go on then, go and get a scarlet handkerchief,' and the blacks were so excited by the scarlet they ran down to the ships like sheep and there they were captured. The Negro has always liked scarlet. It was the fault of this colour that they put them in chains and sent them to Cuba. After that they couldn't go back to their own country. That is the reason for slavery in Cuba. When the English found out about this business, they wouldn't let them bring any more Negroes over, and slavery ended and the other part began: the free part. It was some time in the 1880s.

Because of being a runaway I never knew my parents. I never even saw them. But this is not sad, because it is true.

slave enclosure All the slaves lived in barracoons. These dwelling-places no longer exist, so one cannot see them. But I saw them and I never thought well of them. The masters, of course, said they were as clean as new pins. The slaves disliked living under those conditions: being locked up stifled them. The barracoons were large, though some plantations had smaller ones; it depended on the number of slaves in the settlement. Around two hundred slaves of all colours lived in the Flor de Sagua barracoon. This was laid out in rows: two rows facing each other with a door in the middle and a massive padlock to shut the slaves in at night. There were barracoons of wood and barracoons of masonry with tiled roofs. Both types had mud floors and were as dirty as hell. And there was no modern ventilation there! Just a hole in the wall or a small barred window. The result was that the place swarmed with fleas and ticks, which made the inmates ill with infections and evil spells, for those ticks were witches. The only way to get rid of them was with hot wax, and sometimes even that did not work. The masters wanted the barracoons to look clean outside, so they were whitewashed. The job was given to the Negroes themselves. The master would say, 'Get some whitewash and spread it on evenly.' They prepared the whitewash in large pots inside the barracoons, in the central courtyard.

Horses and goats did not go inside the barracoons, but there was always some mongrel sniffing about the place for food. People stayed inside the rooms, which were small and hot. One says rooms, but they were really ovens. They had doors with latchkeys to prevent stealing. You had to be particularly wary of the *criollitos*, who were born thieving little rascals. They learned to steal like monkeys.

small Creoles

In the central patio the women washed their own, their husbands' and their children's clothes in tubs. Those tubs were not like the ones people use now, they were much cruder. And they had to be taken first to the river to swell the wood, because they were made out of fishcrates, the big ones.

There were no trees either outside or inside the barracoons, just empty solitary spaces. The Negroes could never get used to this. The Negro likes trees, forests. But the Chinese! Africa was full of trees, god-trees, banyans, cedars. But not China – there they have weeds, purslane, morning-glory, the sort of thing that creeps along.

I have never forgotten the first time I tried to escape. That time I failed, and I stayed a slave for several years longer from fear of having the shackles put on me again. But I had the spirit of a runaway watching over me, which never left me. And I kept my plans to myself so that no one could give me away. I thought of nothing else; the idea went round and round my head and would not leave me in peace; nothing could get rid of it, at times it almost tormented me. The old Negroes did not care for escaping, the women still less. There were few runaways. People were afraid of the forest. They said anyone who ran away was bound to be recaptured. But I gave more thought to this idea than the others did. I always had the feeling that I would like the forest and I knew that it was hell working in the fields, for you couldn't do anything for yourself. Everything went by what the master said.

I spent several days walking about in no particular direction. I had never left the plantation before. I walked uphill, downhill, in every direction. I know I got to a farm near the Siguanea, where I was forced to rest. My feet were blistered and my hands were swollen and festering. I camped under a tree. I made myself a shelter of banana-leaves in a few hours and I stayed there four or five days. I only had to hear the sound of a human voice to be off like a bullet. It was a terrible thing to be captured again after you had run away.

Then I had the idea of hiding in a cave. I lived there for something like a year and a half. The reason I chose it was that I thought it might save me wandering about so much and also that all the pigs in the district, from the farms and small-holdings and allotments, used to come to a sort of marsh near the mouth of the cave to bathe and wallow in the water. I caught them very easily because they came up one behind the other. I used to cook myself up a pig every week. This cave of mine was very big and as black as a wolf's mouth. Its name was Guajabán, near the village of Remedios. It was very dangerous because there was no other way out; you had to enter and leave by the mouth. I was very curious to find another exit, but I preferred to stay in the mouth of the cave
in fact they are harmless with the *majases* which are very dangerous snakes. They knock a person down with their breath, a snake breath you cannot feel, and then they put you to sleep to suck your blood.

That was why I was always on guard and lit a fire to frighten them off. Anyone who dozes off in a cave is in a bad way. I did not want to see a snake even from a distance. The Congolese, and this is a fact, told me that the *majases* lived for over a thousand years, and when they got to a thousand they turned into marine creatures and went off to live in the sea like any other fish.

The cave was like a house inside, only a little darker, as you would expect. Ah, and the stink! Yes, it stank of bat droppings! I used to walk about on them because they were as soft as a feather bed. The bats lead a free life in caves. They were and are the masters of caves. It is the same everywhere in the world. As no one kills them they live for scores of years, though not as long as the *majases*. Their droppings turn to dust and are thrown on the ground to make pasture for animals and to fertilize crops.

of slavery

Once I almost set fire to the place. I struck a spark and flames leapt through the cave. It was because of the bat droppings. After Abolition I told a Congolese the story of how I lived with the bats, and the liar – the Congolese were even worse than you could imagine – said, 'A Creole like you doesn't know a thing. In my country what you call a bat is as big as a pigeon.' I knew this was untrue. They fooled half the world with their tales. But I just listened and was inwardly amused.

The cave was silent. The only sound was the bats going 'Chui, chui, chui'. They didn't know how to sing, but they spoke to each other, they understood each other. I noticed that one of them would go 'Chui, chui, chui' and the whole band would follow him wherever he went. They were very united in everything. Bats don't have wings. They are nothing but a scrap of black rag with a little black head, very dark and ugly, and if you look closely at them they are like mice. In that cave I was, as it were, just summering. What I really liked was the forest, and after a year and a half I left that dark place and took to the forest tracks. I went into the Siguanea forests again and spent a long time there. I cared for myself as if I were a pampered child. I didn't want to be taken into slavery again. It was repugnant to me, it was shameful. I have always felt like that about slavery. It was like a plague – it still seems like that today.

To tell the truth, I lived very well as a runaway, hidden but comfortable. I did not let the other runaways catch sight of me: 'Runaway meets runaway, sells runaway.' There were many things I didn't do. For a long time I didn't speak to a soul. I liked this solitude. The other runaways always stayed in groups of twos and threes, but this was dangerous because when it rained their footprints showed up in the mud, and lots of idiots were caught that way.

I had to forage for food for a long time, but there was always enough. 'The careful tortoise carries his house on his back.' I liked vegetables and beans and pork best. I think it is because of the pork that I have lived so long. I used to eat it every day, and it never disagreed with me. I would creep up to the smallholdings at night to catch piglets, taking care that no one heard me. I grabbed the first one I saw by the neck, clapped a halter round it, slung it over my shoulder and started to run, keeping my hand over its snout to stop it squealing. When I reached my camp I set it down and looked it over. If it was well fed and weighed twenty pounds or so, I had meals for a fortnight.

I led a half-wild existence as a runaway. I hunted animals like *jutías*. The *jutía* runs like the devil, and you need wings on your feet to catch it. I was very fond of smoked *jutía*. I don't know what people think of it today, but they never eat it. I used to catch one and smoke it without salt, and it lasted me months. The *jutía* is the healthiest food there is, though vegetables are better for the bones. The man who eats vegetables daily, particularly malanga roots, has no trouble from his bones. There are plenty of these wild vegetables in the forest. The malanga has a big leaf which shines at night. You can recognize it at once.

edible rat

All the forest leaves have their uses. The leaves of tobacco plants and mulberry-trees cure stings. If I saw some insect bite was festering, I picked a tobacco leaf and chewed it thoroughly, then I laid it on the sting and the swelling went. Often, when it was cold, my bones would ache, a dry pain which would not go away. Then I made myself an infusion of rosemary leaves to soothe it, and it was cured at once. The cold also gave me bad coughs. When I got catarrh and a cough, I would pick this big leaf and lay it on my chest. I never knew its name, but it gave out a whitish liquid which was very warming; that soothed my cough. When I caught a cold, my eyes used to itch maddeningly, and the same used to happen as a result of the sun; in that case I laid a few leaves of the *ítamo* plant out to catch the dew overnight, and the next day I washed my eyes carefully with them. *Itamo* is the best thing for this. The stuff they sell in pharmacies today is *ítamo*, but what happens is that they put it into little bottles and it looks like something else. As one grows older this eye trouble disappears. I have not had any itching bouts for years now.

The macaw-tree leaf provided me with smokes. I made tight-rolled neat little cigarettes with it. Tobacco was one of my relaxations. After I left the forest I stopped smoking tobacco, but while I was a runaway I smoked all the time.

And I drank coffee which I made with roast *guanina* leaves. I had to grind the leaves with the bottom of a bottle. When the mixture was ground right down, I filtered it and there was my coffee. I could always add a little wild honey to give it flavour. Coffee with honey strengthens the organism. You were always fit and strong in the forest.

Townsfolk are feeble because they are mad about lard. I have never liked lard because it weakens the body. The person who eats a lot of it grows fat and sluggish. Lard is bad for the circulation and it strangles people. Bees' honey is one of the best things there is for health. It was easy to get in the forest. I used to find it in the hollows of hardwood trees. I used it to make *chanchanchara*, a delicious drink made of stream-water and honey, and best drunk cold. It was better for you than any modern medicine; it was natural. When there was no stream near by I hunted around till I found a spring. In the forest there are springs of sweet water – the coldest and clearest I have seen in my life – which run downhill.

a large conch

I spent most of the time walking or sleeping. At midday and at five in the afternoon I could hear the *fotuto*, which the women blew to call their husbands home. It sounded like this: 'Fuuuu, fu, fu, fu, fu.' At night I slept at my ease. That was why I got so fat. I never thought about anything. My life was all eating, sleeping and keeping watch. I liked going to the hills at night, they were quieter and safer. *Ranchadores* and wild animals found difficulty in getting there. I went as far as Trinidad. From the top of those hills you could see the town and the sea.

The nearer I got to the coast the bigger the sea got. I always imagined the sea like an immense river. Sometimes I stared hard at it and it went the strangest white colour and was swallowed up in my eyes. The sea is another great mystery of Nature, and it is very important, because it can take men and close over them and never give them up. Those are what they call shipwrecked men.

One thing I remember really clearly is the forest birds. They are something I cannot forget. I remember them all. Some were pretty and some were hellishly ugly. They frightened me a lot at first, but then I got used to hearing them. I even got so I felt they were taking care of me. The *contunto* was a real bastard. It was a black, *black* bird, which said, 'You, you, you, you, you, you, you ate the cheese up.' And it kept on saying this till I answered, 'Get away!' and it went. I heard it crystal clear. There was another bird which used to answer it as well; it went, 'Cu, cu, cu, cu, cu, cu,' and sounded like a ghost.

The *sijú* was one of the birds which tormented me most. It always came at night. That creature was the ugliest thing in the forest! It had white feet and yellow eyes. It shrieked out something like this: 'Cus, cus, cuuuus.'

The barn-owl had a sad song, but then it was a witch. It looked for dead mice. It cried, 'Chua, chua, chua, kui, kui,' and flew off like a ray of light. When I saw a barn-owl in my path, especially when it was flying to and fro, I used to take a different way because I knew it was warning me of an enemy near by, or death itself. The barn-owl is wise and strange. I recollect that the witches had a great respect for her and worked magic with her, the *sunsundamba*, as she is called in Africa. The barn-owl may well have left Cuba. I have never seen one again. Those birds go from country to country.

The sparrow came here from Spain and has founded an immense tribe here. Also the *tocororo*, which is half a greenish colour. It wears a scarlet sash across its breast, just like one the King of Spain has. The overseers used to say that it was a messenger from the King. I know it was forbidden even to look at a *tocororo*. The Negro who killed one was killing the King. I saw lots of men get the lash for killing sparrows and *tocororo*. I liked the *tocororo* because it sang as if it was hopping about, like this: 'Có, co, có, co, có, co.'

A bird which was a real son-of-a-bitch was the *ciguapa*. It whistled just like a man and it froze the soul to hear it. I don't like to think how often those creatures upset me.

I got used to living with trees in the forest. They have their noises too, because the leaves hiss in the air. There is one tree with a big white leaf which looks like a bird at night. I could swear that tree spoke. It went, 'Uch, uch, uch, ui, ui, ui, uch, uch.' Trees also cast shadows which do no harm, although one should not walk on them at night. I think trees' shadows must be like men's spirits. The spirit is the reflection of the soul, this is clear.

Translated anonymously from the Spanish
Esteban Montejo

Charles Darwin, Naturalist, Visits a Tropical Forest

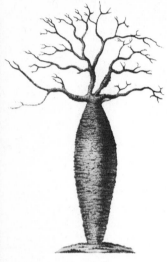

butterflies

Within three days Darwin had arranged to join an Irishman named Patrick Lennon who was about to visit his coffee plantation a hundred miles away to the north. They were a party of seven, all mounted on horseback. In hot sultry weather they followed the coast for the first few days, and then turned inland into the tropical rain forest. To say that Darwin was happy is not enough, he was enthralled, enraptured. All round them vast ceiba trees and cabbage palms, as slender and tall as ships' masts, rose up and with their foliage blotted out the sun. From the topmost branches Spanish moss and long rope-like lianas trailed down through the green light, and in the silence and stillness of the midday heat the great blue morpho butterfly came sailing by. The air was filled with the scent of aromatic plants – camphor and pepper, cinnamon and clove. Then there were the monstrous anthills, twelve foot high, the parasitic orchids sprouting from the tree trunks and the incredibly brilliant birds: the toucans and the green parrots, the tiny humming-bird with its invisibly fluttering wings poised above a flower. Darwin made quick ecstatic jottings in his notebooks as he rode along: 'Twiners entwining twiners – tresses like hair – beautiful lepidoptera – silence – hosannah.'

The blood-curdling cry of the howler monkey erupted through the silence and this was followed by a distant roar like heavy surf falling on a beach – the approach of a storm. Great warm raindrops broke through the canopy of leaves above their heads and in a moment they were drenched. Fresh earthy smells came up into the washed air from the ground, and all the valleys around them were filled with billowing lakes of white mist. Then as the storm passed and it grew dark a tremendous commotion began: the nightly concert of frogs, the cicadas and the crickets, and the flickering of fireflies in the darkness. 'Every evening after dark this great concert commenced; and I have often sat listening to it, until my attention was drawn away by some curious passing insect.'

Darwin and the Beagle
Alan Moorehead

From a Nineteenth-Century Kansas Painter's Notebook

I always paint pictures
of violent weather
(mostly tornadoes
with thick dragon tails
that strike like snakes),
then give them away
to queasy aunts
and quaking uncles.
Though I find peace
in strawberry sunsets,
and those May wine days
when a clover breeze
ding-dongs the tulips,
I am obsessed
with steep funnel-shaped clouds
and frightened children
who cry and run scared
through towering cornfields.
I paint only
the dark-stained pictures
that storm inside my head

Dave Etter

Acknowledgements

For permission to use copyright material acknowledgement is made to the following:

Poems and Prose

For 'O They're Wicked Things' from *I See by my Outfit* by Peter Beagle to Curtis Brown Ltd; for 'The Wildlife of New York' from *The Concrete Wilderness* by Jack Couffer to William Heinemann Ltd; for 'From a Nineteenth-Century Kansas Painter's Notebook' from *Go Read the River* by Dave Etter to the University of Nebraska Press; for 'Observation' and 'The Beach' from *The Unceasing Ground* by William Hart Smith to Angus & Robertson (UK) Ltd; for 'Earthquake' from *The Prodigal Son* by James Kirkup to the author; for 'Cornish Coast' from *The Collected Letters of D. H. Lawrence* to Laurence Pollinger Ltd and to the Estate of Mrs Frieda Lawrence; for 'Glasgow and Salford' from *Streets of Song* by Ewan MacColl and Dominic Behan to Topic Records Ltd; for 'An Ordinary Day' from *Surroundings* by Norman MacCaig to the author and The Hogarth Press Ltd; for 'Charles Darwin, the Naturalist, visits a Tropical Forest' from *Darwin and the Beagle* by Alan Moorehead to Hamish Hamilton Ltd and the author; for 'A Slave Becomes a Runaway' from *The Autobiography of a Runaway Slave* by Esteban Montejo to The Bodley Head; for 'Cave-building' from *Report from a Chinese Village* by Jan Myrdal to the author and William Heinemann Ltd; for 'Once at Piertarvit' and 'The Rain in Spain' from *Oddments, Inklings, Omens, Moments* by Alastair Reid to Laurence Pollinger Ltd; for the extract from the *Revised Standard Version Bible* Ecclesiasticus xliii, 18-20 to the National Council of the Churches of Christ; for 'A Sunny Day' and 'The winter afternoon' from *By The Waters of Manhattan* by Charles Reznikoff to Laurence Pollinger Ltd; for 'Artist's Notebook' from *Selections from the Notebooks of Leonardo da Vinci* edited with Commentaries by Irma A. Richter to Oxford University Press; for 'The Coming of the Cold' from *The Collected Poems of Theodore Roethke* by Theodore Roethke to Faber & Faber Ltd; for 'Thames Scene' from the poem 'Embankment before Snow' from *To Whom It May Concern* by Alan Ross to Hamish Hamilton Ltd; for Lost in the Desert' from *Wind, Sand and Stars* by Antoine de Saint-Exupéry to William Heinemann Ltd; for 'Hats' and 'People Who Must' from *Smoke and Steel* by Carl Sandburg to Harcourt Brace Jovanovich Inc.; for 'Car Fights Cat' from *A Falling Out of Love and Other Poems* by Alan Sillitoe to W. H. Allen Ltd; for 'Lackaday' from *And Another Thing* by Robert Paul Smith to Winant, Towers Ltd; for 'Spring Summer Autumn Winter' by Sydney Smith from *The Weather Eye* edited by C. R. Benstead to Robert Hale & Co.; for 'Waking from a Nap on the Beach' from *Half Sun, Half Sleep* by May Swenson to Charles Scribner's Sons; for 'Sunday Afternoons' from *The Owl in the Tree* by Anthony Thwaite to Oxford University Press; for 'Summer Storm' from *These Happy Golden Years* by Laura Ingalls Wilder to Lutterworth Press; for 'Between Walls' and 'The Winds' from *The Collected Earlier Poems* and 'The Forgotten City' from *The Collected Later Poems* by William Carlos Williams to Laurence Pollinger Ltd.

Pictures For the pictures on pages 2–3, 18–19, 35, 39, 122 to Richard Davies: page 8 to Harry Callahan; pages 11, 14, 15, 16, 17 to The Royal Library, Windsor by gracious permission of Her Majesty The Queen; page 12 to Biblioteca Reale, Turin; page 13 to Biblioteca Ambrosiana, Milan; pages 21, 22–3 to Magnum Photos; page 32 to Jack Couffer; pages 33, 64 to Keystone Press Agency; page 33 to Hanns Reich Verlag; page 36 to Rapho Press Agency; page 38 to Chris Steele-Perkins; pages 40–41, 44–5 to The John Hillelson Agency Ltd; pages 46–7 to George Krause; page 51 to Helen Fisher; pages 52–3 Private Collection; pages 54, 56 to The Library of Congress; page 63 to the US Department of Commerce, Weather Bureau; pages 68–9 to The Bettmann Archive; page 71 to Stern Magazine; pages 72–3 to Camera Press Ltd; page 75 to Novosti Press; page 89 to David Cobham; pages 91, 95 to The Musee de L'Homme, Paris; page 96 to Dr Ahmed S. Fangary; page 112 to The Bodley Head Ltd.

Every effort has been made to trace owners of copyright material, but in some cases this has not proved possible. The publishers would be glad to hear from any further copyright owners of material reproduced in *I Took my Mind a Walk*.